GETTING IN TTOUCH
with
Your Dog

GETTING IN TTOUCH
with
Your Dog

*A Gentle Approach to Influencing Behavior,
Health, and Performance*

LINDA TELLINGTON-JONES
with Gudrun Braun

T

TRAFALGAR SQUARE PUBLISHING
North Pomfret, Vermont

First published in the United States of America in 2001 by
Trafalgar Square Publishing
North Pomfret, Vermont 05053

Published simultaneously in Great Britain by
Kenilworth Press Ltd
Addington, Buckingham, MK18 2JR

Printed in China on behalf of Compass Press Ltd.

Originally published in the German language as *Tellington-Training für Hunde*
by Franckh-Kosmos Verlags-GmbH & Co., Stuttgart, 1999

Disclaimer of Liability
The author and publisher shall have neither liability nor
responsibility to any person or entity with respect to any
loss or damage caused or alleged to be caused directly or
indirectly by the information contained in this book.
While the book is as accurate as the author can make it,
there may be errors, omissions, and inaccuracies.

Library of Congress Card Number: 2001089545

ISBN 1-57076-206-6

Typographic design by Paul Saunders
Layout and typesetting by Kenilworth Press

Contents

To my sister, Robyn Hood,
for her continuous contributions to the development of
TTouch and TTEAM training over two decades.

Illustration Credits

Photos: All photos by Jodi Frediani;
except p.11 by Lothar Lenz; p.3 by Christof Salata;
pp.19, 20 (bottom), 75, 82, 83 by Sandra Wilson;
p.13 by Stevi; and p.15 by Aaron Strong.

Drawings: 7 drawings by Jeanne Kloepfer
(pp.29, 33, 35, 37, 39, 42, 67); 9 drawings by
Cornelia Koller (pp.16, 45, 49, 50, 51, 63, 74, 79,
87); 1 drawing from *Der neue Weg im Umgang mit
Tieren*, Franckh Kosmos, Germany (p.83).

Acknowledgments

My heartfelt thanks goes to my American publisher, Caroline Robbins, for her patience and understanding, for her endless hours of editing, and work on the phone with me discussing the smallest details of the manuscript.

I am grateful to Martha Cook for her support, and for being such fun to work with. My thanks to David Blunt, Lesley Gowers, and others at Kenilworth Press in England for their continuing faith in my work, and to Gudrun Braun, whose concept this book was, and without whom the original manuscript in German would never have been written. Almuth Sieben, you're an angel for continuing to suggest new books.

Thank you, Jodi Frediani, for your photos, and your patience in getting just the right angles. I wish to thank the illustrators Jeanne Kloepfer and Cornelia Koller for their excellent drawings.

In addition, I wish to thank Kirsten Henry for her dedication, patience and attention to fine details of the work, and to Ingrid Winter and Christine Schwartz for their editing contributions. And my deepest appreciation as ever to TTouch instructors Edie Jane Eaton, Jodi Frediani, and Debby Potts, and several hundred TTouch practitioners in twelve countries who continue to bring the work to so many appreciative people and their animals.

Thanks also to the dedicated organization, trainings, and promotion in the German headquarters by Bibi Degn; in England by Sarah Fisher; in Switzerland by Doris Suess; in Austria by Martin Lasser; in Australia by Andy Robertson; and by Eugenie Chopin in South Africa.

My special thanks for their cooperation, patience, and sense of humor at the photo sessions go to the following dog lovers and their dogs: Erika Hull and T-Rex, Mary Ellen Laidlan and Billy G, Jo Buckland and Gimli, Veronica Bridge and Bandit, Lois Shumyk with Tess and Grady, Linda Burnam and Jesse, Adele Getty and Cumae, Sandra Wilson and Griffin, and Uta Henrich.

To my husband, Roland Kleger, for getting me back on course in the last hours of writing when I thought I couldn't finish in time. I must acknowledge our loyal West Highland Terrier, Rayne, who kept me company for so many hours at the computer.

My gratitude to my sister, Robyn Hood, could take a whole page. Robyn was always there for support and brilliant input when I was stuck or needed some creative clarity and encouragement – thank you, thank you.

Of course, I must thank all the dogs that have crossed my trail, or been a part of my life. Without them this book could not have been written.

Introduction

What is the Tellington TTouch Method?

The Tellington TTouch Method consists of three parts: The TTouches; the Leading Exercises; and the Confidence Course.

The History of the Tellington TTouch

Doing bodywork on animals is generally thought to be a modern trend. However, in 1905, my grandfather Will Caywood, a racehorse trainer, having secured eighty-seven wins at the Moscow Hippodrome, was awarded the title of Leading Trainer, and received a prize of a jeweled cane from Czar Nicolas II. He attributed his success to the fact that all the horses in his stable were "rubbed" over every inch of their bodies for thirty minutes each day.

In 1965, my then husband, Wentworth Tellington, and I wrote a book entitled *Massage and Physical Therapy for the Athletic Horse*. It was based on the bodywork done on our horses after 100-mile endurance rides, steeplechases, three-day events, and horse shows—all of which I competed in extensively. We found that our horses recovered much more quickly with bodywork.

However, it never crossed my mind that the behavior and character of an animal, and its willingness and ability to learn, could be influenced by bodywork until 1975 when I enrolled at the Humanistic Psychology Institute in San Francisco in a four-year training course taught by Dr. Moshe Feldenkrais who developed a system of mind-body integration.

My enrollment in this study was an unlikely move on my part. This was a method of working with the human nervous system, and I came from the world of horses. I had been teaching riding and training horses for over twenty years at that time, and for the past ten years had co-owned and directed the Pacific Coast Equestrian Research Farm School of Horsemanship dedicated to the education of riding instructors and horse trainers.

I had signed up for this training hoping I could adapt Dr Feldenkrais' method for humans to enhance my teaching of riding. At that time, I was driven by an intense, intuitive "feeling," which for some inexplicable reason prompted me to take this course. It's almost as if I "knew" that his system, known for increasing athletic ability, alleviating pain, and improving neurological dysfunction

I am doing Leg Circles, which produce a pattern of movement that increases awareness.

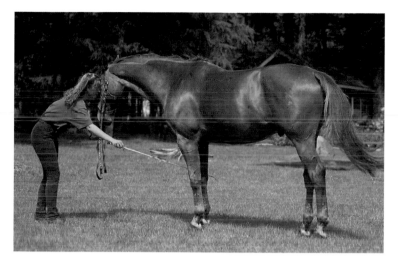

A nervous horse is being invited to lower his head. This lowering action causes him to relax mentally and emotionally.

whether it be from injury, illness, or birth, would become exceptionally effective in improving the performance and well-being of horses.

My epiphany occurred early in July, 1975, as I was lying on the classroom floor with sixty-three fellow students following the instructions of Dr. Feldenkrais. This was only our second day, and we were being guided through a series of gentle movements called Awareness through Movement. He made the statement that a human's potential for learning could be enhanced, and learning time shortened dramatically, by a person moving his own body in non-habitual movements. These movements could be done sitting, standing, or lying down and consisted of exercises that caused parts of the body to experience a new feeling – for example, intertwining the fingers in a different configuration, rather than the usual, comfortable way.

The movements would activate unused neural pathways to the brain, and awaken new brain cells. My first thought was, "What movements could I do with a horse that will be "non-habitual," and will increase a horse's ability to learn?"

Early Bodywork with Horses

That same day after class I went to work on a 16-year-old Arabian mare who was unfriendly around people. She was also difficult to catch, and it took the owner five minutes or so, with the help of some grain, to bring her in. I spent about 45 minutes moving her body around in every non-habitual way I could think of that would feel safe and pleasant to her. I gently moved her lips, ears, legs, and

I am doing some Ear TTouches on this young dog, T-Rex, to calm him down.

tail in ranges and direction she could not move herself. Bringing this new awareness to her body seemed to give her more confidence—definitely making her friendlier – and, at the end of the session, she was very relaxed. I left thinking that what had just happened was extremely interesting.

The next day, the owner called to say that when he went out to catch the mare to bring her in, she immediately came to be caught – most unusual for her. When he took her into the stall she stood close to him as if to say, "how about a little more of that bodywork?" When he told me this, I knew then and there that I was on to something special.

Over the next four years I worked on hundreds of horses developing ways of moving their bodies and working them through obstacles. I saw remarkable improvements in behavior and balance, and experienced a new willingness, and ability, to learn from all of them. I developed this work with horses into a system that came to be known as the Tellington-Touch Equine Awareness Method. We now call it TTEAM, for short.

The Birth of the TTouches

In 1983, the TTouches were born. I was teaching a workshop at the Delaware Equine Veterinary Clinic, staying overnight with one of the veterinarians, and his wife, Wendy. Wendy asked me to look at her Thoroughbred mare that was extremely resistant to being groomed. She would pin her ears, swish her tail, step from side to side, and clearly indicate her displeasure. When being saddled, the behavior was repeated, sometimes accompanied with a raised hind leg, or even a kick.

I began to work on her with Functional Integration – a more advanced Feldenkrais technique. In the case of this mare, I used such light contact and minimal movements that it appeared that my hands were not moving. However, much to Wendy's surprise, the mare began to relax – lowering her head, softening her eyes, and standing quietly.

Wendy could hardly believe her eyes, and asked me, "What is your secret? Are you using energy, or what are you doing?"

Without thinking, I replied, "Don't worry about what I'm doing, just put your hands on the horse's shoulder, and push the skin in a circle." I surprised myself when I said this because, quite honestly, I'm not sure why I did, but I kept quiet, and watched in amazement as Wendy started to push the horse's skin round in small circles with the mare remaining as quiet for her as she had for me. (This wasn't something I had ever done before, and had nothing to do with the Feldenkrais work.)

It was in that moment that I realized something very special had happened. Over the ensuing months – and years – I experimented with various pressures, sizes, and speeds of doing circles. These came to be known as the Tellington TTouches, or TTouches. I used my hands intuitively in many different ways, responding to what the animals liked. My sister, Robyn, who is as observant as an owl, was very helpful in clarifying exactly how I was holding and moving my hands, which gave us specific details about each TTouch.

The TTouches Today

Since that time we have invented over a dozen specific TTouches, each one having a slightly different effect on an animal. As I discovered more TTouches I realized we needed names for them – not just ordinary names, or numbers, but unusual, creative names that would be easily remembered. It seemed logical to name the TTouches for different animals I had worked on – the ones that evoked special memories.

The inspiration for the name of the Clouded Leopard TTouch came from my work with a three-month-old leopard at the Los Angeles Zoo. She had been weaned too early and had developed neurotic habits of sucking her leg, and kneading her paws, for hours on end. I did small circles on her mouth to address her emotional issues, and on her paws to help relax them and bring them more feeling. The "cloud" part of the name describes the lightness with which the whole hand contacts the body (lightly as a cloud), and the "leopard" stands for the range of pressure of the fingers. A leopard can be very light on his feet as in the light TTouch, or very strong as in the higher pressured TTouches.

The Python TTouch was named for Joyce, an eleven-foot-long Burmese Python that I worked on for a demonstration at the 20th annual Zoo Keepers Conference sponsored by the San Diego Zoo in California, in 1987. Joyce suffered from recurring pneumonia every spring. When I first started to work with her, doing tiny circles, she was twitchy and didn't like them, so I intuitively switched to doing slow, small lifts under her body to stimulate her lungs. After a few minutes Joyce stretched out to her full length, and I let her go for a "slither" to get some exercise. When I resumed working on her doing small circles a few minutes later, she relaxed completely and turned to watch me with her nose almost on my hand.

The TTouches build confidence, instill obedience, and develop an animal's ability and willingness to learn. It takes animals beyond

I am doing the Mouth TTouch to reduce stress and neurotic behavior on a serval at the Wild Animal Park in Temecula, California.

I'm using the Mouth TTouch on a macaque to reduce the emotional trauma caused by his being used for psychological research.

instinct, teaching them to think instead of react. It is a system based on gentle circular movements, lifts, and slides done over every inch of an animal's (or human's) body. The intent of the TTouches is to activate the function of cells and awaken cellular intelligence. You can liken it to "turning on the electric lights of the body." A TTouch is done on the whole body, and each circular TTouch is complete within itself. Therefore, it is not necessary to understand anatomy in order to successfully speed up the healing of injuries or ailments, or change undesirable habits or behavior.

The intention is to release pain and fear at the cellular level. When I began to see major changes in the traumatized animals that I was working with twenty years ago, there was little under-standing, and no research, to support what we were seeing. However, neuroscientist, Candice Pert, in her book, *Molecules of Emotion*, has now proven that emotions are held in our cells and transported to our brains by neurotransmitters. I believe that is why the TTouch work has had such success in turning around animals, particularly dogs, that have been abused, and that are timid either from inherited genes or from a lack of socialization.

Over a number of years many people reported success with the TTouches despite the fact that they did not know very much about them, or were even trying them out for the very first time. We do not know exactly why the Circular TTouches are so effective. Perhaps the secret simply lies in a person's mindfulness toward the animal and each circular movement.

Scientists at the Biofeedback Institute in Boulder, Colorado found out that the one-and-a-quarter circles of the TTouch simulta-neously stimulate four different brain waves in humans, and horses. Simple petting, massage, or several circles in one place did not have this effect. They used a machine that had been invented by a scientist, Maxwell Cade. He discovered that this particular pattern of the four brain waves operating simultaneously represents the ideal functioning mode of the human brain, which he called "the awakened mind state." It is the brain wave pattern of highly creative people and healers. Based on Maxwell Cade's observations, and the result of our study with horses, we can assume that the TTouches enhance an animal's ability to learn.

The Tellington TTouch Method with Dogs

Dogs, cats, horses, orangutans, hamsters, snow leopards, elephants, whales, cockatoos, llamas, chimpanzees, the list of animals that have been helped with the TTouch is long and keeps growing. My work has taken me to many parts of the world and I'm constantly learning from my experiences with animals. But, it was my experience with a dog early on that led me to an interesting discovery.

In 1980, I first used the Functional Integration work on an extremely nervous Australian Sheepdog named Shawn. He was a "fear biter," and a chronic, almost unceasing barker. I noticed that when he was barking he walked stiffly with short steps and an extremely high head carriage. By then I had discovered that I could change a horse's behavior by changing his posture. A nervous, tense horse is high-headed. When you teach him to lower his head, which I do with bodywork and through The Labyrinth in the Confidence Course work, he relaxes. When I applied this same technique to Shawn, working his body, ears, and neck in order to get him to lower his head, his breathing slowed down, his stride lengthened and became more fluid, and he relaxed considerably. After a few sessions, to my surprise and pleasure, Shawn's barking came under control, and his tendency to bite reduced. His owner was pleased, and I was thrilled at the prospect of helping this type of problem dog.

Training often seems to be a major challenge for people who have not grown up with dogs. With my background of farm and ranch living (I've had my own dogs since I was eight years old), I took it for granted that a dog would be obedient – would sit, come, and stay when asked. When I recall how cooperative and easy our dogs were to work with I think it happened because I had a clear picture in my mind of what I expected, and my dog "picked up" that picture. I remember taking our five-month-old Great Dane puppy, Tiger, to his first horse show, and asking him to wait patiently by the horse trailer while our horses were groomed and saddled. It never crossed my mind that he would wander away.

World-renowned scientist Rupert Sheldrake, in his fascinating book, *Dogs That Know When Their Owners Are Coming Home,* has finally proved that dogs can read our minds and pick up our mental pictures even when far away. It confirms to me that it was the clarity of my expectations that made my dogs so cooperative over the years, and is the difference between success and failure in so many cases of inappropriate behavior.

In subsequent years the Tellington TTouch has developed into a method that is currently being used by dog owners, trainers, breeders, veterinarians, vet technicians, and in animal shelters in many countries around the world. The TTouch Method offers a positive, no-force approach to training, but is much more than just a training method. With a combination of specific TTouches, Leading Exercises, exercises over obstacles that we call the Confidence Course, you can improve your dog's performance and health,

Here I'm working on Keiko, the orca that starred in the film "Free Willy." Keiko, normally very nervous around strangers, needed to relax and have his confidence increased. He was to be moved to a different location for filming and would be handled by new people. He responded very well to the TTouch and allowed me to work over his whole body.

You will achieve best results if you perform the Circular TTouches in connected lines along the body. When you have finished making one circle, slide your hand lightly to the next circle position.

solve common behavioral issues, and positively influence physical problems. You can use it to assist with recovery from illness or injury, or enhance the quality of your animal's life. Many people discover a deepened rapport with their dogs, and reap the reward of non-verbal, interspecies communication.

The Tellington TTouch Method can help dogs with cases of excessive barking and chewing; leash pulling; jumping up; dog-aggressive behavior; fear-biting; timidity and shyness; resistance to grooming; hyperactivity and nervousness; car sickness; hip dysplasia; fear of thunder, and loud noises. It also helps problems associated with aging such as stiffness and arthritis, and many other common behavior and physical ailments. In this book, behavior and physical problems together with recommended TTouches are listed in chart form to make it easy for you to see at a glance. However, in many cases involving behavior issues, if you do any three of the TTouches all over your dog's body, and add a few short sessions over the Confidence Course, you will experience an improvement in behavior. The charts are here to give you some tips, but once you have practiced, learn to trust your feeling and instinct and just follow your fingers.

The Tellington TTouch Method, developed with the assistance of my sister, Robyn Hood, continues to spread around the world helped by ten books in eleven languages, twenty-three videos, countless magazine articles, a bi-monthly newsletter, and numerous television documentaries and radio programs in Europe, Australia, and the U.S. There are over 200 certified practitioners in twelve countries teaching the work for dogs in workshops and individual sessions. You can find the practitioner closest to you by contacting the TTEAM offices, and if you have questions, or would like to share a TTouch story with us for others to read in our newsletter, contact us at the addresses provided at the back of this book.

Try the TTouches Yourself

It is well known that massage can relax the muscles. TTouch takes this concept one step further. Your dog can begin to learn and cooperate in a new way and a few short treatments can produce permanent changes in personality. Doing only two to ten minutes of TTouches a day can achieve unexpected results. Many people have found that after a while their dogs begin to demand their daily TTouch sessions.

The wonderful thing about the TTouches is that you do not need to perform the circles perfectly in order to be successful. Neither do you need to know the anatomy of the body, as you do when performing massage. You also do not have to try the various TTouches all at once. Instead, you can start with a few and gradually add more to your repertoire. I usually suggest you start with the Lying Leopard TTouch or the Clouded Leopard TTouch. Try to find those TTouches that your dog enjoys the most.

When you start doing a TTouch make sure that your fingers are relaxed and that you move the skin with light pressure. Each TTouch consists of a one-and-a-quarter circle. When you are finished with one circle, slide your hand to a different place, and start another TTouch. In this way you draw lines of connected circles along the dog's body. Be sure to perform each circle very gently. Experience has shown that gentle, light contact is more effective than strong pressure.

The Canine Golden Rule

Dogs enrich our lives in so many ways with their gifts of unconditional love, friendship, and loyalty. You can reciprocate by being mindful of our Canine Golden Rule: Treat your dog, as you would like to be treated. Using the TTouch methods you can "reshape" your dog's behavior with kindness and a level of understanding, which you will find carries over in your attitudes toward your family, and even yourself. It encourages you to open your heart to encompass a happy, healthy relationship with your dog, as well as members of your own species.

Through the Circular TTouches, you can deepen your connection with your dog, while at the same time enhancing his ability to learn.

A Vet's Point of View

Martina Simmerer, a veterinarian who works at an animal clinic near Salzburg, Austria, has been using The Tellington TTouch Method for more than ten years. In 1990, she began her training with me to become a TTouch practitioner. In recent years she has been teaching a seminar at the University of Vienna Veterinary School called "Bodywork and Behavioral Therapy for the Horse." This seminar is based on the TTouch Method. Dr Simmerer writes:

“ I had just started veterinary school when I first heard about the Tellington TTouch Method. The reason why I took my first class was because of a problem horse that did not respond to any conventional method of treatment. When I found out how quickly I was able to help that horse with the Tellington TTouch, I was totally fascinated. I realized right away that I had finally found the method of working with animals that I had been searching for for years.

However, I was trained in the sciences, and hence skeptical. I have to test a new approach in order to see whether it really is as valuable as it seems at first sight. While I was a student I was taught to question everything and to observe carefully. Consequently, I documented my progress with my first study group and kept a detailed TTouch training diary. Later, when I had more experience, I started a TTouch work group with my students at the veterinary school. The University of Vienna has always been blessed with open-minded professors. For example, acupuncture has been taught there for many years, and in 1989 and 1990, Linda Tellington-Jones was a visiting professor at the Department of Orthopedics. That department also hired me in 1998 to teach an elective course called Bodywork for Rehabilitation and Behavior Modification. Twenty-four students completed the course. ”

Ear TTouches can save an animal's life when it goes into shock.

Use of the TTouches in a Vet's Practice

Martina Simmerer continues:

“ You should always be aware that your safety is most important. A dog in pain can snap, or bite, by reflex at any given moment even if he is usually extremely mellow. This is why in a potentially dangerous situation you should use a muzzle, or have another

Touching a dog's body with a wand is an excellent way of making contact with a fearful, or aggressive dog.

person restrain the dog safely. It often happens that people concentrate so hard on doing TTouches that they forget to pay attention to their own body language. You should avoid any gesture or body position that may seem threatening. For example, do not lean over a dog or stare one directly in the eye.

- To make contact with a nervous animal use random, one-second Clouded Leopard TTouches. This allows you to gain a dog's trust and make the examination easier.
- If there are areas on a dog's body that he won't let you touch or treat, use the Raccoon and Clouded Leopard TTouches in connected lines.
- The TTouch not only helps an animal 'release' his fear and tension, but it is also an excellent aid for treating pain. Injury healing can be accelerated with the TTouch – wounds heal a lot faster, comparable to a successful laser treatment. However, hands are always 'at hand' and are a lot less expensive than complicated machines. Wounds must, of course, be cleaned, disinfected, and often sutured and bandaged. After this has been done perform Raccoon or Lying Leopard TTouches with extremely gentle pressure around and on the bandaged area.
- Animals with arthritis, spondylitis, or degenerative hip disease respond well to supportive TTouch treatments. The diagnosis of incurable joint disease is very frustrating to a veterinarian and, especially, to a dog's owner. With the TTouches, an owner can be empowered to alleviate his or her dog's pain and to minimize the use of drugs.
- Properly performed, the Tail TTouch helps with problems in the

The Zigzag TTouch is one of the Connecting TTouches.

Robyn Hood, my sister, is demonstrating the Lying Leopard TTouch on her dog, Shawnee.

The Body Wrap helps fearful, and/or hyper-active dogs to feel more secure about their bodies.

spine and the intervertebral disks.
- For dogs of large, fast-growing breeds that tend to have problems with growth and coordination, the TTouches can improve the connection from the front to the back of the body. The Zigzag TTouch, Tarantulas Pulling the Plow, and Connected Circles, are all especially helpful.
- Many dogs suffer from recurrent tooth and gum diseases, such as plaque, tartar, inflamed gums, and even cavities. Good preventive care includes a special diet and regular tooth brushing, which is a lot easier if the animal is used to the Mouth TTouch.
- You will quickly win over the heart of a dog by gently massaging the animal's ears. This is one of Linda Tellington-Jones' most important discoveries. The Ear TTouch should be a regular part of the veterinary repertoire because it can save a life. It is extremely useful in a case of shock – after an accident – in circulatory failure, in heatstroke, after anesthesia, as well as in a case of fright from less dramatic situations such as carsickness. "

Leading Exercises and Groundwork in a Vet's Practice

Dr Simmerer goes on:

" Veterinarians are often asked questions about animal behavior. The ground exercises with 'non-habitual' movements (the Feldenkrais concept described in the Introduction) enhance an animal's physical and emotional balance. This work greatly improves concentration and coordination, and changes the learned behavior patterns of animals as well as humans. The goal of the ground exercises is to bring the dog's body into balance, and to provide the animal with an enjoyable and stress-free experience of his own body. Eventually, the dog will be able to act consciously rather than react instinctively.

An excellent aid to solving many problems is the correct use of the Halti, or a similar head collar (p.76). We always use the Halti in combination with a flat collar (not a choke chain, or choke collar), or a harness, in order to avoid any damage to the dog's cervical vertebrae. It is a well-known fact that the conventional method of 'correction,' a jerk on a choke chain, can seriously damage a dog's neck and larynx.

The Body Wrap (p.82) gives fearful and hyperactive dogs a subtle framework, and helps them feel more secure. Child psychologists use similar 'wrapping' techniques to treat panic attacks, for example. "

The Experience of a Dog Trainer

Stevie Avastu is a behavior consultant and dog trainer in Great Britain. She is famous for her success with aggression, and other behavioral problems. Many dogs of various breeds are trained for Schutzhund (protection) work with the wrong methods, and are not reliable around people. Often Stevie is the last resort for such dogs and their owners and trainers. She writes:

" I first learned about the Tellington TTouch Method in the early 90s from participating in a weekend workshop. I found the ideas interesting, but also a little 'crazy,' and did not try them myself. In the summer of 1996, I found out that Linda Tellington-Jones was going to give a class in my area, so I decided to take it. When the day was over, I was fascinated by what I had seen and learned. Linda's demonstration kindled my interest and motivated me to finally try the TTouch work. Since then I have taken advantage of every opportunity to learn more about it.

Many dogs with all kinds of issues are presented to me. Some are like a whirling dervish, others are shy, and others aggressive. The common denominator in most of these cases is stress. Stress prevents an animal from learning new lessons. This is the reason why the calming effect of the TTouches is so useful. Again and again, I find that a 20-minute session of the TTouches suffices to relax a dog's tense body. Tension gives way to calmness and receptivity, and the dog becomes more attentive.

As stress diminishes, the dog's self-confidence increases. The dog is now able to change unwanted behavior patterns. When the owner performs bodywork on the animal the relationship between the two of them improves. This is a very important step toward success because I am only a mediator – it is the owner who has to take the dog home and teach him new behaviors.

The ground exercises are extremely valuable in various ways. The dog learns to pay attention to different tasks. Fear is 'released' as the dog learns to concentrate on a specific exercise. His coordination and rhythm improve, which is very important for competitions and agility training. In addition, the groundwork helps to balance the dog, which means that he learns to stand and sit in his own balance without pulling or leaning into a person. In other words, the dog learns to take responsibility for his own behavior. This is the key to dealing with behavioral issues. "

The Mouth TTouch affects the limbic system – the part of the brain that controls emotions.

I demonstrate the Ear TTouch.

FERN, A GERMAN SHEPHERD

❝ Fern, was a 22-month-old female German Shepherd that had longstanding problems with aggression. Before she was brought to me she had attacked a neighbor. She seemed fearful when she entered my living room and sat down next to her owner, watching me with her head raised high.

I decided that Fern was a good candidate for TTouches and asked the owner if I could put a Halti on her. The owner held Fern while I began to work on her body. I felt that one to two minutes of TTouches, followed by a five-minute break, was enough for this dog. After several two-minute sessions the owner was able to let go while I was working on Fern's lips and gums. Then, I left the room. The owner reported that while I was gone the dog stood right by the door watching it closely. She tilted her head and wagged her tail. This was something she normally did only when her owner left the room. When I returned I sat down on the sofa and called Fern. She came to me wagging her tail, put her front legs on my legs, and licked my face. We were amazed.

Doing some TTouches are certainly a great way to introduce yourself to a dog. I know of no other way to make contact so quickly. Petting a dog the way most people do just does not have the same effect. ❞

Test Your Dog – The Checklist

Does Your Dog Have One of the Following Problems?

You can solve many typical behavior problems with the TTouches. The purpose of the list below is to help you identify your dog's behavior and health status. The column on the right refers to the TTouches and exercises you can try. Of course, these TTouches do not replace veterinary care. However, you can use a TTouch (or TTouches) to help your dog on the way to the vet, to prevent some diseases, or to support the vet's treatment of an injury or illness.

Behavior and health check	This is what you can do
Your dog is/has:	
Afraid of strangers, or the vet	Ear TTouch, Lying Leopard TTouch
Afraid of loud noises	Tail TTouch, Mouth TTouch, Body Wrap, Ear TTouch
Urinating when scared or excited	Ear TTouch, Tiger TTouch
Barking uncontrollably	Halti, Ear TTouch, Lying Leopard TTouch, Mouth TTouch, Tail TTouch, Python Lifts
Hyperactive	Combined TTouch, Clouded Leopard TTouch, Zigzag TTouch, Body Wrap, Halti, Ear TTouch, Mouth TTouch
Nervous before competitions	Ear TTouch, Mouth TTouch, Combined TTouch, Lick of the Cow's Tongue
Fearful and insecure	Ear TTouch, Mouth TTouch, Leg Circles, Tail TTouch, Body Wrap, Clouded Leopard TTouch
Shy	Lying Leopard TTouch, Tail TTouch, Mouth TTouch, Body Wrap
Chewing on objects	Mouth TTouch
Aggressive toward other dogs	Halti, Clouded Leopard TTouch, Body Wrap, Leading Exercises with other dogs
Aggressive toward cats	Halti, TTouches simultaneously with a cat, Body Wrap, Calming Signals
Pulling on the leash	Halti, Leading Exercises, Balance Leash, Clouded Leopard TTouch, Leg Circles
Lagging behind on the leash	Halti, Double Diamond, Leading Exercises, Body Wrap, Ear TTouch, Combined Lying Leopard with Python Lift

Vomiting in the car	Ear TTouch
Nervous and upset in the car	Ear TTouch, Halti, Body Wrap, Combined TTouch
Unhappy when groomed	Tarantulas Pulling the Plow, Hair Slides, TTouch with a sheepskin, Combined TTouch, Abalone TTouch
Unwilling to be bathed	Ear TTouch, Combined TTouch, Hair Slides, Leg Circles before and during the bath
Difficult to nail trim	Python TTouch on the legs, Raccoon TTouch on the paws and nails, Leg Circles, TTouch with the paw
A fresh injury	On the way to the vet: Ear TTouch, gentle Raccoon TTouches around the injury
A wound that is healing	Raccoon TTouch, Lying Leopard TTouch around the wound
Surgery	Ear TTouch, Lying Leopard TTouch before and after
A fever	On the way to the vet: Ear TTouch
In shock (after an accident, for example)	On the way to the vet: **first** do Ear TTouch, **later** Lying Leopard TTouch on entire body
Arthritis	Python TTouch, Raccoon TTouch, Ear TTouch, Body Wrap
Hip Dysplasia	Daily Raccoon TTouch on the pelvis, Python TTouch, Tail TTouch
Teething	Mouth TTouch with a cool washcloth
Indigestion	Ear TTouch, Belly Lifts, Lying Leopard TTouches on the belly
Colic	On the way to the vet: Ear TTouch, Belly Lifts
Sensitive ears	Llama TTouch, Lying Leopard TTouches with a sheepskin, Circles on the ears while supporting the head
Stiff joints	Python TTouch, Combined TTouch
Difficulty getting up, and going up and down stairs	Body Wrap, Belly Lifts, Python TTouch, Tarantulas Pulling the Plow, Tail TTouch, Ear TTouch, Lick of the Cow's Tongue
Allergies	Bear TTouch, Ear TTouch, Clouded Leopard TTouch
Itching	Tiger TTouch, Bear TTouch

Your female dog is/has:

Breathing difficulties	Ear TTouch, Tail TTouch, Combined TTouch on the back legs, Clouded Leopard TTouch
Pregnant	Belly Lifts, Lying Leopard TTouch and Combined TTouch on the belly, Raccoon TTouch, Ear TTouch, Tail TTouch
Giving birth	Ear TTouch, Lying Leopard TTouch, Python TTouch, Combined TTouch
Not accepting her puppies	Ear TTouch, Lying Leopard TTouches with a warm washcloth on the nipples, Mouth TTouch

Your male dog is/has:

Aggressive toward other males	Halti, Labyrinth, Wand, Leading Exercises with other dogs, Journey of the Homing Pigeon, consider castration

Your puppy is/has:

Not nursing	Mouth TTouch, Ear TTouch, gentle TTouches on the tongue, Lying Leopard on the whole body
Teething	Mouth TTouch
Needs toenails trimmed	Python TTouch on the leg, Raccoon TTouch on the paws and nails
In the socialization learning phase	Mouth TTouch, Ear TTouch, Clouded Leopard TTouch, Tail TTouch, TTouch on the paws

The TTouches

You can reduce stress and strengthen the immune system with the Ear TTouch.

Shawnee is relaxing and enjoying Tarantulas Pulling the Plow.

Why TTouch?

"The Tellington TTouch Method is like a non-verbal language." This is how I like to define the TTouch in a few words. As I said earlier, the goal of the TTouch bodywork is to stimulate the function and vitality of the cells in an animal's body, and to activate unused neural pathways to the brain. In the research we've done, it has been shown that circular movements simultaneously activate all four types of brain waves. In addition, stress-reducing hormones are released. Further positive effects of the TTouches are that your understanding of your dog is enhanced, he gains trust in you, as well as confidence in himself. There is a boost in the dog's health and general sense of well-being. Some of the TTouches may look like a kind of massage technique; however, their purposes are not only to relax muscles, but also to produce changes in behavior.

Pressure Scale

Since our main goal is to activate cells and neural pathways rather than relax muscles most of the TTouches are performed with less pressure than you might expect. I have developed a scale in order to help you understand the various pressures. First, try these variations in pressure on yourself in order to get a clear idea of the feeling.

• To find the lightest pressure, rest your thumb against your cheek to support your hand. With the tip of your middle finger push the skin on your eyelid around in a circle and a quarter, with the lightest possible contact. This is a Number One, or lightest pressure. (If you wear contact lenses, do this TTouch test above your eyebrows.)

• Now try the Number One pressure on the fleshy part of your forearm and note the mark on your skin. Go back to your eye and this time push the skin on your eyelid around in a circle as firmly as is comfortably possible. This is a Number Three, or medium, pressure.

• Repeat the Number Three pressure on your forearm

again and note the depth of indentation into the muscles. For a Number Six, or heaviest pressure, you would double the Number Three pressure (and see a corresponding indentation), though a Number Six pressure is rarely used on dogs.

• Watch your dog's reaction to the TTouch and adjust the pressure accordingly. Normally I use Number Three or Four pressures for areas that are neither sensitive nor painful. Sensitive areas are treated with the lightest pressure of Number One or Two.

Safety Tips and More

If you are TTouching your own dog you should know him or her well enough to not be afraid of any sudden or unexpected reactions. Nevertheless, you should be careful, and especially so if you are working with a strange dog that is fearful or aggressive.

• Never look a frightened or aggressive dog in the eye. Dogs feel threatened by this. Always approach a strange dog from the side and begin your TTouches in this position.

• Be quick to respond to any negative reaction. Reduce the pressure, or change to a different area of the body if you notice that the dog is uncomfortable.

• Some dogs like to lie down while being TTouched, while others feel safer standing or sitting. Make yourself comfortable as well – keep your wrists straight and relaxed, and breathe regularly.

• Support your dog's head with one hand if you are working on the head. For dogs with hip or back problems it eases the pressure in these areas if you put your hand or knee under the dog's abdomen when he is standing.

• You can stabilize the head of a restless dog by hooking your thumb in his collar.

Most TTouches are performed with light pressure.

You can stabilize a restless dog with your thumb in his collar.

The Clouded Leopard TTouch

Enjoyable, relaxing, and confidence-building

The Clouded Leopard TTouch is the basic TTouch. All the other Circular TTouches are variations on the Clouded Leopard TTouch. To perform this TTouch your fingers should be slightly curved with the pads of your fingers close together. Depending on your dog, you can apply a very light, or a slightly deeper pressure. With regular work your dog will develop more trust and willingness to cooperate. This TTouch has proven especially effective for nervous and anxious dogs. It can also help dogs feel more confident in new and challenging situations such as obedience training or competitions.

WHAT IT LOOKS LIKE

HEAD TO BACK

If you do Clouded Leopard TTouches all over your dog's body you will make him more aware of it as well as enhance his feeling of well-being. Begin at the center of the head and do connected TTouches in a straight line across the neck, shoulders, and along the back. Continue with similar lines of connected TTouches parallel to each other.

FRONT AND BACK LEGS

Tense, anxious, or shy dogs can gain self-confidence through TTouches on their legs. They also become more connected to the ground. Start at the upper part of the leg and move down toward the paw. Try to space your circles evenly. Your dog can stand or lie down, whichever position is most comfortable for him.

HOW TO

Place your hand (with your fingers slightly curved) on your dog's body. Keep your fingers lightly together and move the skin around in a one-and-a-quarter circle. The darkened areas of the fingers as shown in this drawing should be in contact with your dog's skin. Your thumb rests on the dog's body and establishes a connection with your other fingers. Keep your wrist as straight and flexible as possible. Your fingers, hand, arm, and shoulders should be relaxed. Put your other hand on your dog's body as well; this will help you maintain your balance. Start at 6 o'clock, and push the skin clockwise until you reach 6 o'clock again, then go on to 8 or 9 o'clock. The normal speed for completing one circle is two seconds, using a pressure of Number Two to Four. As soon as you are finished with one circle connect it to the next one by sliding along the fur to your next position running parallel to the spine or down the legs.

PAWS

Through the Clouded Leopard TTouch on the paws your dog will become grounded and sure-footed. This work also prepares your dog for having his nails trimmed. Use a medium pressure of the fingers to perform this TTouch on the paws.

WHAT YOU SHOULD DO IF...

...the dog doesn't like a TTouch, or moves away

If your dog is nervous or very young you may have to contain him gently in the beginning so that he cannot move away. Your dog may also be calm in the beginning but try to get away from you as soon as you start working on him with TTouches. There are many possible reasons for this. It could be that the pressure is too heavy, that your fingers are stiff, you are holding your breath, you are doing too many circles in one place, or your dog is sensitive to any touch in a particular area. Try a different TTouch, slow down your speed, change the pressure, or move to an area that the dog will accept.

In the Clouded Leopard TTouch the circular movement is done with the fingertips.

Case History

Bella, a Great Dane, with Mobility Problems

Patty Dykes writes:

" A breeder of Great Danes asked me for help because he was worried about his 11-month-old bitch named Bella. Her back was arched high and when she walked, she crossed her right hind leg in front of her left one. In addition, she had lost almost 18 pounds in two weeks and only moved when she was asked. She became aggressive when anyone tried to touch her.

A vet had advised the owner to have Bella X-rayed in order to find the cause of these symptoms. However, two sets of complete X-rays did not reveal anything out of the ordinary. The breeder was sent home with some medication and was asked to return to see the vet if he did not see any improvement.

At that time Bella's helpless owner called me and asked me to take a look at his dog. When I did, it seemed to me that one of the reasons for her problem with mobility was her extremely tense muscles.

For safety, I asked the owner to hold Bella while I began doing TTouches on her back legs. First, I did Lying Leopard TTouches on the inside of her cramped and tense back legs in order to relax the muscles and to gain her trust. Then I did light Clouded Leopard TTouches on the outside. When I felt her muscles relax somewhat, I stopped and asked the owner to walk the dog for a few steps. To his and my amazement she walked perfectly.

I showed the breeder how to do these TTouches and recommended regular sessions with Bella several times a week. He called me a few days later and told me that Bella was doing very well. He continued working with her like this and she became a healthy, normal dog. "

Case History

Wizard, a St Bernard, Who Has Arthritis

Eleanor Blancanelle Gardiner writes:

When doing the TTouches, you should always support the dog's head with your other hand.

66 About two-and-a-half years ago Linda gave a workshop for horses in our area. At the same time my St Bernard, Wizard, had a bad attack of arthritis in his neck. He was unable to bend it, and when he tried, he whined in pain. He was able to eat and drink only when lying down. Linda suggested I treat him with Clouded Leopard TTouches. Later the same evening, I started doing the TTouches on Wizard. I began behind his ears and later worked along the sides of his body all the way to his tail. I performed TTouches in connected lines along his body.

The next morning Wizard came running toward me, tail wagging, as if he were asking me for more TTouches. Since that day his arthritis has never returned with such severity. Several times a year, whenever the weather is changing, Wizard comes to me and "demands" a TTouch session.

Wizard asks for his TTouch sessions even before the stiffness in his neck is at all apparent to me. This may be the reason why his arthritis has improved so much. Wizard and I are grateful to Linda Tellington-Jones. 99

The Lying Leopard TTouch
For deeper connection

To do the Lying Leopard TTouch, flatten your hand softly on the body allowing a larger area of warm contact. Move the fingers of your flattened hand with light pressure. This gentle, relaxing TTouch creates a bond of trust between you and your dog.

WHAT IT LOOKS LIKE

HEAD AND NECK
Almost all dogs enjoy having their heads touched and petted. However, if your dog is fearful he may not like to be touched in this area. Build his trust with gentle Lying Leopard TTouches on his forehead, on the sides of his mouth, under his muzzle, on his neck, and on his entire body.

SHOULDERS
Tension in the shoulder muscles will restrict your dog's freedom of movement and his breathing. Through the warmth of your hands you can relax these muscles and reduce fear, nervousness, and hyperactivity.

WHAT YOU SHOULD DO IF...

...the dog wants to get away

Concentrate on the TTouches and do not let external things distract you. Pay attention to making your circles even and round and keep your fingers soft and flexible. Change the direction of the circles to counter clockwise to see if that helps him settle down. In the beginning, some animals find these more enjoyable and relaxing. After a while however, you should be able to do the clockwise circles. Or, try the suggestion on page 35 under "what you should do if your dog doesn't like the TTouch."

THIGHS AND LEGS

You can help a dog with hip problems, tired muscles after intensive training, or one that is afraid of loud noises, by doing Lying Leopard TTouches on the outside and the inside of the thighs. Start at the top of the thigh and do Lying Leopard TTouches in lines of connected circles all the way down to the paws. Pause for two seconds at 9 o'clock at the end of doing the circle-and-a-quarter.

HOW TO

Put your hand on the dog's body and move the skin with your flattened fingers in a one-and-a-quarter circle. Look at the drawing: all shaded areas of the hand should normally be in contact with the body, but in some cases (when TTouching your dog's head, or a leg, for example) do not try to place the heel of your hand on the dog because your wrist would not stay straight. Rest your other hand on the dog's body. Start at 6 o'clock and push the skin, usually in a clockwise direction, one-and-a-quarter times. Your thumb rests on the fur and maintains a connection with the other fingers. I recommend doing the circles slowly and with light pressure. Normally, a circle should take about two seconds. When you are finished with one circle connect it to the next one by sliding your hand over the coat to the next position a few inches away.

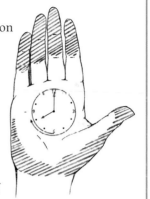

The Python TTouch
Relaxes and stimulates circulation

The Python TTouch is especially helpful for shy, tense, and insecure dogs. Fear and tension reduce self-confidence and impede circulation. Doing the Python TTouches on your dog's legs can improve his circulation and, consequently, his confidence. For hardworking dogs—search-and-rescue, and assisted therapy dogs, for example—the Python TTouch softens tense and sore muscles. This TTouch also improves a dog's mobility, balance, and gait. You can do the Python TTouches on the shoulders, back, and abdomen. The pictures show how to do Python TTouches on a dog's legs.

WHAT IT LOOKS LIKE

FRONT LEGS

Approach your dog from the side and place your whole hand around the leg just below the elbow. When you are working with a large dog you can use both hands; with a small dog you can use just your fingers. After the first Python TTouch, slide your hands down and do another one. Continue in this manner until you reach the paws.

UPPER PART OF THE HIND LEGS

Encircle the thigh with your flat hands, placing your thumbs on the outside of the thigh. For safety, only bend over a dog if you know him well and are sure that he will not snap or bite. Python TTouches in this area are especially helpful for dogs that are afraid of loud noises.

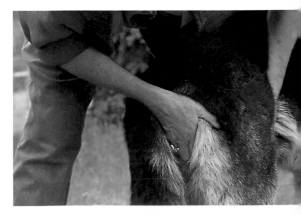

WHAT YOU SHOULD DO IF...

...the dog does not want to be TTouched

In extreme cases, for example if a dog snaps or bites, you can use a wand to get him used to being TTouched. The wand allows you to keep a safe distance. If the dog is non-threatening, but appears uncomfortable with contact, use the back of your hand, or a mitten made out of sheepskin or soft fabric.

LOWER PART OF THE HIND LEGS

Since the diameter of the lower part of the back legs is much smaller you can encircle it with both hands or with just one hand. Do the Python TTouch in whichever way is most comfortable for you and your dog. When you have reached the paws and are finished with the leg, do a Noah's March on the entire leg from top to bottom.

HOW TO

Python TTouch

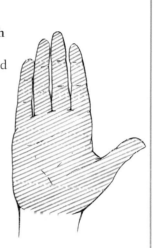

Place your whole, flat hand on the body. Gently and slowly move the skin and muscle upward. Breathe with the movement and hold for a few seconds. With your other hand you can hold your dog by his collar, or you can hold and stabilize him on his chest. Without changing the contact or pressure, slowly return the skin to the starting point. If you spend twice as much time on releasing the skin as on lifting it, the relaxing effect will be greater. When you perform Python TTouches on the legs, slide down an inch or two after each lift until you reach the paws. When working on the body, do the Python TTouches in equal distances and in parallel lines.

Combined TTouch

This TTouch is a combination of the circular TTouch and the Python TTouch. The circular movement enhances awareness, and the lift relaxes, increases circulation, and deepens breathing. At the end of a circular TTouch push the skin straight up at 9 o'clock and let it down again slowly. Inhale with the lift and exhale with the release.

The Abalone TTouch

For sensitive, fearful, and sick dogs

Because the contact with your completely flat hand provides warmth and security, this TTouch is ideal for sensitive, sick, or injured dogs. You can also help nervous animals calm down and relax. Dogs that are very sensitive to being touched or brushed can overcome their fear and resistance with the help of the Abalone TTouch..

HOW TO

To do the Abalone TTouch, place your flat hand on the dog's body. Your whole hand moves the skin in the usual one-and-a-quarter circle. It is important that you use just enough pressure so that your hand does not slide over the surface of the skin but actually moves it. The Abalone is very similar to the Lying Leopard TTouch, but since the whole hand pushes the skin in a circle (instead of the fingers), it is easier to do.

WHAT IT LOOKS LIKE

SHOULDER

The Abalone TTouch is great for calming nervous dogs and for relaxing tense and painful muscles in a dog's shoulders. The warmth of the hand contributes greatly to this effect. If your dog lies down (like Robyn's dog, Shawnee, in the picture) you can reach both shoulders easily.

The Llama TTouch

For dogs that do not like to be touched

The Llama TTouch is performed with the back of the fingers. Sensitive, and fearful dogs perceive the touch of the back of the hand as less threatening. With dogs like these, use this TTouch at first. Once they begin to trust you, you can use other TTouches.

HOW TO

For the Llama TTouch use the back of your hand, or fingers, to make the one-and-a-quarter circle. The pressure is always light. It can be applied using the knuckles only, or with the entire hand. As usual, start at 6 o'clock, and push the skin around in a one-and-a-quarter circle.

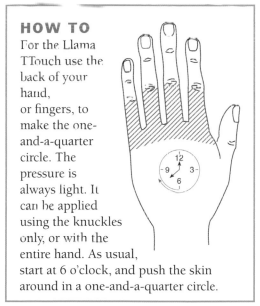

WHAT YOU SHOULD DO IF...

...the dog refuses to be touched

The Llama TTouch is often appropriate here. Many dogs are afraid that open hands could grab them, so it's a good idea to always first touch a fearful dog with the back of your hand. This is much less threatening, and many nervous dogs then readily accept a soft touch.

WHAT IT LOOKS LIKE

FLANKS

Dogs who are afraid often tremble, and are very tense. In this picture, I am gently holding Bandit, a Jack Russell Terrier, by the shoulder. While talking to him in a soothing tone of voice I stroke his side with the back of my hand (the Llama TTouch) to help him release tension.

The Raccoon TTouch

For injured, swollen, sensitive areas of the body

The small, light circles, called the Raccoon TTouch, are useful for reducing any swelling, soreness from hip dysplasia, and sensitivity in a dog's pads or nails. You can reduce pain in a short period of time if you apply the lightest possible pressure. Moreover, with the Raccoon TTouch you can speed up the healing process and bring more awareness to the affected area of the body.

WHAT IT LOOKS LIKE

BACK AND THIGHS

I recommend very light Raccoon TTouches for pain and tension in the back or thighs as tense muscles can make your dog nervous or hyperactive. Some dogs that have injured a leg develop a habit of favoring it even after it has healed. When this happens you can often reeducate the nervous system by using Raccoon TTouches. You release the memory of the pain at a cellular level and increase the dog's awareness that the leg is now healed and is safe for him to put his weight on it.

TAIL

In this picture, I am using my right hand to make very light Raccoon TTouches on a docked tail while holding my left hand on the dog's spine. Amputated tails and legs can cause lifelong phantom pain. You can erase such memories of pain and eliminate a feeling of insecurity by touching the end of the stump with many tiny, very light circles. Moreover, docked tails are often very tense and the Raccoon TTouch can ease this tension. In addition, when a docked tail is long enough, you can gently hold the other side of the tail with your thumb to make a connection between your fingers and thumb.

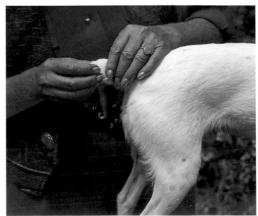

HOW TO

Bend the tips of your fingers at a 90-degree angle and move the skin in a tiny one-and-a-quarter circle. This TTouch is done with very light pressure. When a docked tail is long enough, you can gently hold the other side of the tail with your thumb to make a connection between your fingers and thumb.

You can also do the Raccoon TTouch without using your thumb. On many areas – the leg or the head, for example – there is not enough room to place your thumb on the dog's body. Put your other hand close to the first one to help balance and stabilize your dog's body. When a dog is fidgety and will not stand still, hook your thumb in the collar to keep him quiet. Be aware of the roundness of your circles. Approximately one second for each circle will give the nervous system time to record the contact helping to release the memory of the trauma caused by the tail docking.

TAIL

This photo shows a different way of doing the Raccoon TTouch on a dog's tail. I am supporting underneath the dog's torso with my left hand. You can see that the muscles on the back and thighs are very relaxed. This helps make the Raccoon TTouch on the tail more effective.

WHAT YOU SHOULD DO IF...

...the dog won't stand still

You can let your dog sit, or lie down, if he does not want to stand. However, if he is restless you can hook your thumb into the back of his collar to contain him.

Doing Raccoon TTouches on the tail can help a dog overcome fear and insecurity.

Case History

Melanie, a Neglected Golden Retriever

Barbara Pennisi writes:

" I adopted Melanie about three years ago from a shelter. She had been living by herself in a swamp for quite a while and had become somewhat wild. Her behavior was hardly that of a family pet.

When I adopted her I was unable to touch her ears, legs, or tail. If I tried to touch her tail she snapped. However, I felt that if I could only touch her I would be able to win her heart. TTouch was the key.

I re-read all the articles on TTouch I had, and tried to apply the information to Melanie. I followed my intuition and did Circular TTouches, Ear TTouches, and Connecting TTouches on her entire body.

It took several treatments, but soon Melanie relaxed. Nowadays, Melanie enjoys the TTouch and grooming, and obeys me absolutely. She just glows with joy and happiness, and has become my closest friend. "

Raccoon TTouches are helpful for dogs who have extremely sensitive paws ...

Case History

The Weak Puppy

Linden Spear writes:

❝ I had a litter of ten puppies. One of them was noticeably smaller than the rest. He was weak, and had no nursing reflex. It is possible to raise such a puppy with a bottle. However, he should also get his mother's milk, which contains important antibodies.

I tried to put this puppy's mouth to a nipple but he just would not suck. I did Raccoon TTouches on his face and muzzle, and worked his ears. The TTouches stimulated the puppy and he began to nurse.

For the first two weeks he was only able to nurse if I did the TTouch on him. I gave him milk replacer in addition to his mother's milk and continued TTouching him. I tried Leg Circles, Python TTouches, Tarantulas Pulling the Plow, and Circular TTouches in order to stimulate his entire body. After two weeks this puppy was able to nurse without the help of the TTouch.

Since he was still smaller than his siblings, I continued to give him the milk replacer until he was able to eat puppy food. Fortunately, he was able to stay with his littermates until weaning. Most weak puppies have to be separated from the litter in order to survive and as a consequence of such isolation often have problems with socialization.

I am sure that it was only through doing the TTouch that I was able to save this puppy's life and to let him grow up with his family. ❞

... and pads.

The Bear TTouch
Heals itchy areas

For the Bear TTouch, hold your fingers at a 90-degree angle to the body and make the circle with your fingernails rather than with the pads of your fingers. The difference between the Raccoon TTouch and the Bear TTouch is that the Raccoon TTouch is performed with the fingertips while the Bear TTouch is done with the fingernails straight into the body.

HOW TO

With the first joints of your fingers press straight down into the skin. Make your one-and-a-quarter circle mainly with your fingernails. If you are working on a heavily muscled area, roll the skin with your nails and fingertips over the muscle and make a tiny circle. Hold your fingers close together. In order to do the Bear TTouch effectively, your fingernails should be of medium length, somewhere between one-eighth and one-quarter-of-an-inch. Try the Bear TTouch on yourself first to see how much you can feel your nails. The pressure should vary between Numbers 1 and 4. You may want to place a damp, cool cloth over an irritated and itchy area and do the Bear TTouch through the cloth. Apply only slight pressure – Numbers 1 to 3 – on insect bites, areas of skin allergies, and hot spots.

WHAT IT LOOKS LIKE

FLANKS AND BACK

It is very important to work with just the lightest pressure. The improvement is not caused by the pressure, but by the heightened awareness in that area of the body.

The Tiger TTouch
Soothes skin and calms a dog

If you want to soothe a large itchy area, or calm a hyperactive, heavily muscled dog, use the Tiger TTouch. You can also use this TTouch when you start working with a restless animal.

NECK AND BODY

You can use the Tiger TTouch on almost any area of the body. If your dog is nervous and restless make your circles fast at first; then slow down and watch for the animal to calm down. On itchy areas and hot spots make the circles slowly and use a light pressure that is acceptable to your dog. If the hot spot is irritated or open, place a clean cloth over the area and do the TTouches through it.

HOW TO

When doing the Tiger TTouch hold your hand like a big paw. Keep your fingers curved and separated by about one-half inch. Bend your fingers in such a way that you can feel the skin under the fur with the tips of your fingers. Keeping the same distance between the fingers make a one-and-a-quarter circle with each finger simultaneously. Your thumb should not make a circle but maintain a steady connection with the body. Place your other hand on your dog's body to keep him still.

WHAT IT LOOKS LIKE

Tarantulas Pulling the Plow
Desensitizes skin and stimulates circulation

The Tarantula TTouch is a variation on an ancient Mongolian method called "skin rolling." It releases fear, reduces touch sensitivity, and stimulates circulation. Thus, it is helpful for dogs that are nervous when touched, and dogs that have limited body awareness. You can also increase your dog's trust in you. Try the Tarantula TTouch on yourself, or on another person, to experience its relaxing effectiveness.

WHAT YOU SHOULD DO IF...

...the dog does not like to be TTouched on his hindquarters and growls

Start instead at the neck, and move toward the tail. Use less pressure than before and slow down. It could be that your dog's hindquarters are painful or that he is scared. Therefore, it might be helpful to try a different TTouch at first or to touch your dog gently on the hindquarters with a wand. You can also make circles on your dog's hindquarters with the button end of the wand.

WHAT IT LOOKS LIKE

1. Place your hands at the tail end and work up to the dog's head. Move your fingers against the lay of the coat for improved circulation, but if your dog is nervous, start at the head instead and move backward to the tail.

2. The index fingers and middle fingers of both your hands "walk" forward activating neural impulses, while your thumbs create a raised furrow of skin.

HOW TO

Place your hands side by side on your dog's body. The tips of your fingers should "walk" forward in the direction of the movement while your thumbs point to the side and lightly touch each other. Take a "step" of about one inch with both index fingers simultaneously and allow the two thumbs to follow behind like a plow. The skin in front of your thumbs will be rolled gently. Next, take a step with the middle fingers. Your index fingers and middle fingers alternate in making steps while the thumbs are pulled along. All this should be done with an even, flowing motion. Run several of these "lines" from tail to head on different areas of your dog's back parallel to his spine.

3. Walk your fingers like a spider along the fur while keeping your thumbs to the middle. In this way you move your fingers over your dog's back and head all the way to the tip of his nose.

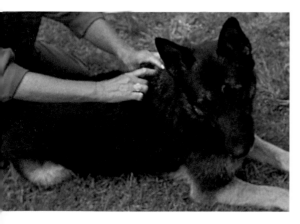

Case History

SIMBA, AN 8-YEAR-OLD MALE COLLIE, SUFFERING FROM PARALYSIS

Simba's back legs were partially paralyzed after a car accident. There was hope that the paralysis would reverse. Simba's owner had heard about the TTouches from his vet. He tried out different ones, hoping that he might be able to help his dog. After several TTouch sessions he noticed that Simba seemed to become a bit more mobile after the Tarantula TTouch, and visibly enjoyed it. Encouraged, he continued the stimulating Tarantulas along with other TTouches, and, miraculously, after several months of work, Simba walked again.

Hair Slides
Relaxing

Doing Hair Slides is an excellent way of making a connection with your dog since they are relaxing for both of you. It provides a pleasant experience that is helpful with dogs that are afraid of being groomed.

WHAT IT LOOKS LIKE

HEAD

Most dogs like slow, gentle Hair Slides on their heads. With this TTouch you can calm down a nervous or fearful dog, and build a special relationship. Hair Slides are also helpful for dogs that suffer from panic attacks or dogs that bark or whine constantly. Keep your dog's head still by placing one hand under his muzzle.

SHOULDERS

Dogs that pull on the leash, or that are hyperactive, nervous, or high-strung, are usually very tense in the shoulders. Try these Hair Slides to relax them. Hair Slides done on a large area with the fingers of your flat hand lead to deep relaxation. Support the opposite shoulder with your other hand. On longhaired dogs, separate your fingers and glide upward through the fur.

WHAT YOU SHOULD DO IF...

...the dog's hair is too short to do Hair Slides

Lift your dog's skin up gently with your thumb and index finger and slide along the hair while letting go of the skin very slowly.

HOW TO

Hold a small tuft of hair between your thumb and index finger, or use the spaces between the fingers of your flat hand, to gently slide up from the root of the hair to its end. Start as close as possible to the roots of the hair and follow the lay of the fur. If you do your Hair Slides slowly and gently, you will build a calm, deep relationship with your dog. Note: on a longhaired dog, run your fingers through his hair with a gentle pull as you might run your fingers through your own hair.

BACK

Hair Slides can be an enjoyable introduction to TTouch bodywork for dogs that do not readily accept other TTouches. Hair Slides on a dog's back create more awareness and flexibility in a gentle and loving way. You can work the large areas of the back with your whole hand, and smaller areas with your fingers.

Case History

MAXI, A NEGLECTED MALE DOG, ABOUT THREE YEARS OLD

Maxi was found as a stray and brought to an animal shelter. His long fur was completely matted. Since the dog was very scared, shaving him was not an option. His new owner tried to straighten out the matted hair by hand. By doing Hair Slides he was able to win the dog's trust and prepare him for brushing and a partial shave. Maxi was TTouched before and during brushing; afterwards the owner did gentle Hair Slides as well. Each step of the grooming process was deliberately kept short in order to minimize the stress on Maxi and to make the de-matting possible. Many groomers have discovered the value of using TTouches to reduce stress and relax dogs that resist being groomed.

Lick of the Cow's Tongue

Increases body awareness and stimulates circulation

The Lick of the Cow's Tongue is a long, diagonal stroke across a dog's body. It is relaxing, stimulates circulation and improves an animal's sense of his own body. Dogs especially enjoy this TTouch because it is performed gently across, or against, the lay of the hair. You can improve your dog's sense of well-being by covering large areas of his body as you move your hand from his belly to his back, or across both shoulders.

WHAT IT LOOKS LIKE

The Lick of the Cow's Tongue connects a dog's entire body from belly to back, and from head to tail. Moreover, it stimulates the circulation. I start at the end of the dog's back and slide my hand, fingers spread slightly, against the lay of the hair. Gimli, a male mixed-breed dog, is enjoying this TTouch very much–he is holding his head low and his tail is relaxed.

I am sliding my hand slowly along Gimli's back and up to his shoulders. My left hand steadies him; my wrist is straight, with fingers relaxed and spread out, so I can glide my hand gently and smoothly through his fur.

I am finishing the Lick of the Cow's Tongue at the dog's head, right between his eyes. The next strokes should also be done along his whole body, alternating between the right and left side of the spine.

Case History

PAUL, A HUSKY MIX, WITH A SORE BACK

Paul was often hard to motivate in agility classes. Because of his stiff back he was not able to negotiate some of the obstacles as fast as other dogs. Through bodywork, especially the Lick of the Cow's Tongue, his back became more flexible. Also, when Paul's owner came to realize that his problems were physical rather than mental as she had first thought, she became less demanding of him. Consequently, Paul became more cooperative and happy to perform in training classes and competitions.

WHAT YOU SHOULD DO IF...

...the dog will not lie down for this TTouch

You can do Lick of the Cow's Tongue with your dog standing or sitting until he learns to enjoy it and lies down on his own. Make sure that your hands are soft and gentle, and remember to breathe slowly and evenly. Using a grooming table is another option to consider.

HOW TO

1. Start at the belly and slowly slide your hand upward through the fur. Your fingers should be curved and slightly spread apart. Note: I am lightly holding the dog's collar with my left hand.

2. Glide your hand upwards keeping your fingers relaxed. The movement should be as fluid as possible.

3. After the first stroke, move your hand toward the dog's hindquarters by a distance of about the width of your hand, and then repeat the procedure until you've covered the whole body. Include the legs and shoulders.

4. The drawing shows another possible direction of the stroke to use if your dog is on a grooming table. The distance between the strokes depends on the size of the dog. Be sure to cover the whole body.

Noah's March

Used to start and close a TTouch session

Noah's March is the TTouch we use to start and to close a session. To begin, you can also use these long, calming strokes with the lay of the fur to acquaint yourself with a dog, and, at the end of a TTouch session, the sweeping strokes along the entire body connect all the areas that have been worked on. The Circular TTouches awaken the cells in specific areas of the body. With Noah's March you can re-integrate the areas that were worked on.

HOW TO

Follow the contours of the body with your flat and soft hands. Use long, sweeping strokes and keep your fingers relaxed. When you start working with a new dog, establish contact with a few calm, slow, and short Noah's March TTouches. When you work with this dog approach him from the side rather than head on, and talk to him in a calm, soft voice. When you close a TTouch session, work in long, slow, sweeping strokes on the body. Make sure you cover every inch of his body and tail, and work all the way down the legs to the end of his paws.

The Zigzag TTouch

Stimulates the body and improves circulation

The Zigzag TTouch is a variation of the Lick of the Cow's Tongue. Because of the changes in direction you stroke the dog both with, and against, the lay of the fur. The Zigzag TTouch is also a good way to get the attention of nervous and hyperactive dogs. When done slowly it calms, and when done more quickly, it activates the neural impulses.

HOW TO

The name of the Zigzag TTouch indicates how it is done. With your fingers spread apart, move your hand in a line interspersed with several sharp angles along the body. Your hand slides with, as well as against, the lay of the fur. Your wrist should be straight, and your fingers spread and relaxed. If you are working with a restless dog, move your hand fast at first, and gradually slow down. Make quick strokes if you want to wake up a lethargic dog.

Start with the Zigzag TTouch at the shoulder, and move your hand up and down over the ribs and along the body all the way to the thighs.

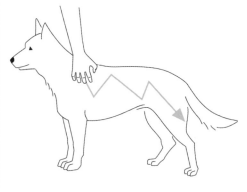

The Belly Lift
Reduces stress and tension

Belly Lifts help dogs relax their abdominal muscles, and take deep breaths. They are especially effective for digestive problems and nervousness. Pregnant bitches usually enjoy this TTouch; moreover, the Belly Lift is useful for dogs with stiff or sore backs, and dogs that have a problem getting up from the floor.

WHAT IT LOOKS LIKE

BELLY LIFT WITH YOUR HAND
Put your left hand under the abdomen and your right hand on the back of your dog. With your left hand apply pressure toward the spine, but only to the extent that your dog is comfortable. Hold this position for about six seconds then slowly release the pressure. The slower you release, the more effective this TTouch will be.

BELLY LIFT WITH A TOWEL
Gimli is lying on his side while I perform Belly Lifts with a towel. (Gimli's owner, Jo, is doing the Mouth TTouch on Gimli's lips to relax him.) Pull the towel under the dog's body so that the center of the towel is under his belly. Lift and release very slowly.

HOW TO

You can perform the Belly Lift in various ways, as these photos demonstrate. Whichever method you use, it's important to work slowly. For example, you may gently lift the animal's abdomen with a towel in six seconds. Hold this position for another six seconds before releasing the pressure very slowly taking about ten seconds. The slow release is of utmost importance for getting the desired effect. Start on the belly right behind the elbows and move toward the hindquarters by the width of your hand, or the towel, for each subsequent lift.

If you do Belly Lifts while you are standing, make sure you protect your own back. In the photo on this page, Mary Ellen and I demonstrate how to do this. I am standing by the side of the dog and supporting my elbow with my hip, while Mary Ellen is turned toward the dog with her legs in the position of taking a step and her knees slightly bent. You can also do Belly Lifts by yourself using your hands. Make sure that your movement comes from your pelvis, knees, and feet in order to protect your back.

BELLY LIFT WITH A TOWEL AND TWO PEOPLE

With a larger dog, Belly Lifts are best done with the dog standing. Mary Ellen is holding the towel, while I am gently pulling as far as Billy finds it comfortable. Mary Ellen and I start at the rib cage just behind the front legs and move toward the hindquarters by the width of the towel for each subsequent lift.

Case History

SHAWNEE, A BELGIAN TERVUREN, WITH WEAK HIPS

Shawnee, Robyn's dog, has weak hips and very straight back legs, which makes it difficult for her to get up from the floor. X-rays show that she has calcium deposits in the joints. In order to keep her pain at a minimum, Shawnee favors her hind legs, and as a result, gets tense in her back. Robyn helps her dog to relax these muscles by regularly performing lifts with a towel on Shawnee's hind legs. She pulls the towel between the hind legs taking the weight off the dog's hips just as in a Belly Lift. Robyn treats both sides and is able to relax the muscles and alleviate the pain. Of course, this TTouch does not replace veterinary treatment but it is something you can do to help your dog and reduce pain.

The Mouth TTouch
Influences emotion

The TTouch on the lips and in the mouth activates the limbic system – the part of the brain that controls emotion, and is the center of learning. The Mouth TTouch is thus helpful for all dogs, but especially for those that suffer from fear, stress, nervousness, and hyperactivity. It also works well for chronic barkers. It sounds amazing, but many dogs that act aggressively toward other dogs respond positively to the Mouth TTouch and, as a result, change their behavior.

WHAT IT LOOKS LIKE

ON THE LIPS
Here, Robyn demonstrates a variation of the Mouth TTouch. She puts her hand under the muzzle and performs light Circular TTouches on the outside of Shawnee's lip.

ON THE GUMS
Robyn gently pushes her thumb under the lip and uses it to do Circular TTouches on the gums. In this way she can easily reach the gums of the upper and the lower jaw.

WHAT YOU SHOULD DO IF...

...the puppy won't let you touch his mouth

Some puppies will not hold their heads still, or want to chew your fingers when you try to do the TTouch on their mouths. Puppies have very sharp teeth, so it is a good idea to wear leather gloves. Stay at the puppy's shoulder and hook your thumb in his collar in order to contain him.

With one hand encircle the muzzle by supporting the lower jaw with your fingers and placing your thumb gently, but firmly, on top of the muzzle. Use your other hand to hold the muzzle in a similar way. With your thumbs, do soft Raccoon TTouches on the outside of the lips and on the gums. In this position you limit the movement of the puppy's head. It is important to keep this exercise short and to repeat it several times. Despite initial resistance, if you quietly persevere your puppy will soon learn to accept and enjoy this TTouch.

...the dog is aggressive

If you are working with an aggressive dog you should do the Mouth TTouch only if you can be sure that the dog will not bite you. Watch his body language very carefully. With a dog that is known to be "people-aggressive" I recommend that you contact a practitioner who has experience with such dogs. Do not attempt to work with an aggressive dog by yourself. (You may find that using the knob of the wand wrapped in an ace bandage will allow you to work the gums and lips from a safe distance.)

HOW TO

1. Here you can see the muzzle of a very relaxed dog named Billy. I begin with Lying Leopard TTouches on the dewlap. With my other hand, I am supporting the dog's head.

2. I slowly move my hand toward Billy's nose and do gentle Lying Leopard TTouches in order to accustom him to having the outside of his mouth TTouched.

3. Finally, my fingers slide under the lip along the gums in gentle Lying Leopard TTouches. I am using the thumb of my other hand to carefully push his lip up.

Lying Leopard TTouches help to get a dog used to having his mouth TTouched.

Case History

Kaisa, a Toy Poodle, with seizures

Laura Mancini writes:

" Three years ago, Kaisa, my six-year-old female toy poodle was kicked by a horse. As a result, she had convulsive seizures two or three times a month. During the seizures her back and neck became completely stiff, and her legs jutted out from her body at weird angles while her head slowly rolled from side to side. Despite the fact that she was fully conscious, she was totally uncoordinated and unbalanced. She was able to look at me, lick her lips, and swallow. These seizures lasted about 20 to 30 minutes. Afterward, it took her about an hour to get back to normal.

Three weeks ago, when she had another seizure, I started to do quiet, Lying Leopard TTouches immediately working on her ears and mouth and along her back down to her pelvis. Within five minutes the seizure was over. I kept her close to me for a few minutes until she grabbed a toy and ran around the house.

The next morning, I was woken up by a wet nose. It was Kaisa. She was having another seizure, but only a very mild one. The only sign of it was the fact that her head was trembling. I immediately did the TTouch on her ears and mouth and within three minutes the seizure was over.

Prior to this incident Kaisa had never had such a short and mild seizure, and no drug had produced such a positive result. Since then I have been doing the TTouch with Kaisa everyday, and there have been no signs of a seizure. Moreover, Kaisa's hips and back seem to have become more stable. The end of next week will mark Kaisa's first seizure-free month! "

Case History

Gayla, a Komondor, with cancer

Jodi Frediani writes:

Gentle circles on the gums improve a dog's health.

" For six months Gayla had been suffering from a fast-growing mammary tumor. One week after a hospital stay I wanted to bring her into the house because she was sleeping in the rain under a tree. She was unable to climb the stairs so we went to the back of the house where I put her into a basket on the porch. The next day it was still raining and Gayla left her place only to eat and to defecate. The morning after that she could hardly move and took no interest in her environment. She got up only when I asked her to, and was obviously in pain.

I started to do the TTouch on her ears, around the base of the ears, on her head, and on her legs. After about 15 minutes she was more alert, her pain seemed to diminish, and she was able to get up and walk around. Two days later she was almost her old self – she stayed at the fence barking at strangers.

One week later, Gayla woke me up during the night. She was whining as she changed her position or tried to get up. I sat down with her and started to TTouch her ears and head. I was crying, and Gayla put her head on my shoulder. Her breathing slowed down and I told her that I thought it was time for her to go. As I continued doing Ear Slides she relaxed her neck completely and put her head in my lap. She had never done that before and I felt that she wanted to tell me that she agreed with me. It is important to mention here that Gayla had always been a very independent dog who had little need for physical contact. On the following morning we ended her suffering. Through the TTouch I was able to make a deeper connection with my dog than ever before. The TTouch also helped me make the difficult decision to put Gayla to sleep. "

The Ear TTouch
Calms and soothes

The Ear TTouch is the most effective way to calm a hyper-active dog. Dogs who have been introduced to the Ear TTouch often "demand" it from their owners. It has been known for many centuries that working the ears of humans has a positive effect on the entire body and its organs. This principle is applied successfully in acupuncture. The Ear TTouch is especially important in cases of shock when the circulation may be breaking down. Doing Ear Slides immediately after an accident, or before and after surgery, stabilize circulation.

WHAT IT LOOKS LIKE

Stabilize the dog's head with one hand. The thumb and the fingers of your other hand hold the opposite ear in such a way that your thumb is on top. Change hands when you want to stroke the other ear. Gently stroke the ear with your thumb from the center of the head to the base of the ear and all the way to the tip. Work different areas with each slide so that you cover every square inch of the ear. With a floppy-eared dog, lift the ears gently so they are horizontal to the ground. Work upright ears in an upward direction.

If your dog has soft, floppy ears support the ear with your fingers. Do not pull the ear but just stroke the fur gently. Imagine the ear to be a rose petal so use only the lightest pressure. If you are trying to help a dog that is in pain or in shock, you may want to make your strokes faster and apply slightly more pressure. If you are trying to help your dog relax, use slow and gentle slides.

WHAT YOU SHOULD DO IF...

...the dog has pointed ears

If your dog has stiff, pointed ears you need to stroke the ears in the direction they grew – upward.

HOW TO

1. Even long ears should be stroked *horizontally* all the way to the tip. In this picture, Gimli is lying on the floor and is very relaxed. I am holding his muzzle and stroking his ear with my right hand.

2. You can also make small circles with your thumb in order to cover the entire surface of the ear. Hold the ear out sideways and start at its base. This circular Ear TTouch helps the dog with arthritis.

3. Work the whole surface with small, light TTouches until you arrive at the lower edge of the ear.

Case History

Purzel, a West Highland Terrier, ten years old, suffers from carsickness

He hated riding in the car. He became very upset as soon as he realized that he had to get in because he had often vomited when it moved. However, when his owner tried Ear TTouches before and during a trip, he relaxed, and the carsickness disappeared.

The Ear TTouch: Stroke the dog's ear from its base to its tip.

Case History

A Golden Retriever who is frightened of thunderstorms

Judy Hodge writes:

" Last summer I was able to help a female Golden Retriever overcome her fear of thunderstorms. One day I was watching the dog and her owner – our neighbor – sitting on the lawn. I noticed that the dog was completely rigid, her muscles were tense, and her whole body was trembling. I could hear the sound of thunder in the distance and I saw the dog's tension growing with the approaching storm.

We asked the dog to lie down and I did TTouches on both ears. After a while she began to breathe normally and was able to relax between the thunderclaps. Finally, she stayed calm even during the loudest roar. After thirty minutes the storm had passed. By that time the dog was very relaxed and almost asleep.

After the next storm I asked my neighbor how the dog had done. I was happy and a little surprised when I heard that his dog had hardly paid any attention to the storm. She was lying down peacefully the whole time and stayed relaxed in spite of the thunder.

Even now, one year later, the dog continues to remain calm during thunderstorms and even fireworks – all this the result of only thirty minutes of the Ear TTouch! I can certainly recommend TTouches to all readers whose dogs are afraid of thunderstorms. "

(Despite Judy's success with just thirty minutes of TTouches, some cases may take three or more TTouch sessions between thunderstorms, and also the use of the Body Wrap, p.82.)

Case History

Ricki, an Australian Shepherd, has difficulties when whelping

Linden Spear writes:

Ear TTouches stabilize blood pressure.

" Ricki's first whelping was not easy. Already twelve hours before the first puppy was born she was suffering from the strain of the contractions. She was so exhausted that she fell asleep sitting up, and only woke up each time she lost her balance. After thirty-six hours of labor, she was completely exhausted.

The next time I decided to help Ricki relax during the whelping process by doing the Ear TTouch. I had heard that with this TTouch it was possible to support a bitch in labor. It really seemed to work for her. In addition, at a point when Ricki started to shake uncontrollably, I put her in my lap and worked her entire body with TTouches. She stopped trembling. I also did Belly Lifts with a towel and Python TTouches on her legs to ease the birthing process. The TTouches really helped her relax and avoid the usual terror and panic. She also seemed better able to focus her energy on giving birth. It turned out to be an easy whelping and she had eleven puppies that she raised with special care.

Her reactions to my attempts to help her were very different from the first whelping. I noticed that she actually seemed grateful to me during this whelping. I now use the TTouch on all my bitches to support them before, and during, birth. "

Leg Circles with the Front Legs

Improves balance and gait

Circles on the front legs will help your dog gain a new awareness of his limbs, and will increase his range of motion. You can relax his neck and shoulder area and enhance his sure footedness, especially if he is very tense. Leg Circles also help nervous animals – dogs that are scared of loud noises and thunderstorms, and those who are anxious about slippery surfaces.

WHAT IT LOOKS LIKE

Your dog should be relaxed and lying on his side. Support the dog's elbow joint with your right hand. With your left hand, hold the paw and bend it at the wrist. Circle the paw slowly a few times in each direction.

With your right hand, move the leg from the shoulder forward and simultaneously open the wrist so that the leg lies almost straight in your hand.

WHAT YOU SHOULD DO IF...

...the dog will not relax his leg

It may be a new experience for your dog to allow his legs to be moved in an unusual (non-habitual) way. Give him time to get used to this new sensation, and work without using force or pressure. If he pulls his leg away just gently go with him and make him feel comfortable. When you sense that he is relaxing somewhat, try doing the Leg Circles again. It is often helpful to do a few Circular TTouches along the leg before you begin with Leg Circles. Also, some dogs are very ticklish on their paws, which is why they pull their feet away. In these cases hold the leg on the joint above the paw, rather than the paw itself.

Now move the leg back to its original position in one slow, fluid motion with movement coming from the shoulders.

HOW TO

You can do Front Leg Circles with your dog standing, sitting, or lying down. It is essential that you do not force the movement. The dog should release his limbs to you and relax his muscles. Try to produce an easy, small movement. Do not strain, or even stretch, any of the joints. If your dog tries to pull his leg away don't grab it, just go with it and try again. Often it helps to gently push the leg in the direction that the dog is pulling and then do the Leg Circles from the new position. You may also find that you can move one leg more easily than the other. Such a difference can be the result of chronic tension, or an old injury, which you can remove by doing tiny Leg Circles regularly.

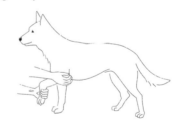

Leg Circles with the Hind Legs
Improves balance and coordination

With these Hind Leg Circles you can show your dog his freedom of movement and teach him new ways of using his body. Working and Sporting dogs gain more awareness of their bodies and learn to use them more efficiently. Hind Leg Circles also relax the muscles all the way to the back, which helps calm nervous dogs and those afraid of loud noises.

WHAT IT LOOKS LIKE

While supporting the leg above the ankle with one hand, I am holding the left flank with my other hand. With the bent leg make small circles in both directions. Make sure not to twist the joints, especially if the dog has had an injury. I do not recommend doing these Leg Circles with dogs who suffer from hip dysplasia, knee injuries, or arthritis.

Here, I'm supporting Bandit with one hand on his chest while I move his hind legs with my other hand. The diameter of the circles should be easy for the dog to maintain his balance. You should not feel any resistance. Move the leg in a smooth, fluid motion.

WHAT YOU SHOULD DO IF...

...the dog cannot balance on three legs

Either work with your dog in the lying-down position, or support him under the belly so you can help him find his balance standing. Then start by lifting a leg for a moment and putting it down again. When he feels more secure, do small, round circles with the paw.

...the dog favors a leg

Leg Circles improve balance, especially after an injury. They help dogs that are partially paralyzed, or ones that are favoring a leg – after surgery, for example. Often, an injury has healed completely, but the memory of the pain remains in the cells so favoring that leg becomes a habit.

HOW TO

1. Your dog can be standing or lying down while you stand or sit behind him. When he is laying down support the dog's knee with one hand. With the other, lightly hold the leg above the paw.

2. Now, carefully move the leg back from the hips. You will know by your dog's reaction what is, or what is not, comfortable for him. Stretch the knee joint so that the leg is almost straight.

3. Finally move the leg forward and bring it back to its original position. Repeat these movements so that they resemble the fluid motion of running.

TTouches on the Paws
Overcome fear of toenail trimming

TTouches on the paws are especially effective for dogs who refuse to have their paws touched, who have sensitive paws, or who are afraid of having their toenails trimmed. They are also helpful for dogs that panic when faced with unusual surfaces such as slippery floors or unfamiliar stairs.

WHAT IT LOOKS LIKE

Start at the top of the paw with Raccoon TTouches. Take the paw in one hand and, with the other hand, do as many TTouches close together as possible. Continue all the way down to the nails.

On the bottom of the paw start with light Raccoon TTouches on the pads. Put your fingers in the spaces between the pads and make small circles.

WHAT YOU SHOULD DO IF...

...the dog growls when you get close to his paws

Be cautious and go back to work on a place he accepts. Then using a piece of sheepskin, do Connected Circles along his leg. The next step is to touch the dog's other leg with his paw (see TTouches with the Paw, p.68). You can also offer your dog some treats to make the experience more pleasant.

Finally, do TTouches on each toenail. If your dog remains relaxed during this treatment he will be prepared for toenail trimming. However, if your dog is afraid of nail clippers, use the clippers to do circles on his body.

HOW TO

Your dog can sit, lie down, or stand. Do some of the TTouches your dog enjoys the most in order to relax him. Then, starting at the top of the leg, do Clouded Leopard TTouches all the way down to his paw. Do gentle Raccoon TTouches on the paw, covering the whole area. The shaded portion of the hand in this drawing shows you how you use only the tips of your fingers for the Raccoon TTouch. If your dog is ticklish between the pads work with less pressure on these areas. If your dog has long hair between the pads, he may be extra ticklish, so you may want to trim the hair first before attempting to trim his nails.

TTouches with the Paw

Reduces sensitivity

The idea of TTouching a dog with his own paw seems strange at first sight, especially since the area of the body that can be reached with a paw is not very large. But, the goal of this exercise is to reduce the sensitivity of the paws and make your dog feel safe so that it will be easier for you to work on them regularly. Try it and you may be surprised by the result.

HOW TO

1. I have bent Bandit's leg so that I can make circular movements on his other leg with my hand under his paw. Look at Bandit's face. He is looking slightly skeptical and unsure about what is happening and is turning his head to investigate.

2. Billy does not seem to know what is happening to him, either. He is licking his lips – a sign of insecurity. I am doing TTouches with his paw on his other leg from top to bottom.

Toenail Trimming
A stress-free procedure

It is important to trim a dog's nails regularly if he does not wear them down. Toenails that are too long can badly affect a dog's posture: instead of putting his weight on the entire paw he will shift it to the back of the pads. This unnatural position can lead to soreness and tension throughout the dog's body.

HOW TO
With some exceptions, the nails should be short enough so that you do not hear them click on a hard floor. However, be careful not to cut the nails too short. With a difficult dog you may need another person's help. Only cut a few nails at a time, and give your dog several breaks. It is often easier if you cut his nails while the dog is standing.

WHAT IT LOOKS LIKE

I have won Gimli's trust with 15 minutes of bodywork. Here, I am introducing Gimli to the nail-clipping procedure by making Circular TTouches with the clippers on his leg.

With lots of Raccoon TTouches on the paws and nails, I have thoroughly prepared Gimli to have his feet and paws handled. Thus, Gimli hardly reacts when I take one of his nails between my fingers.

I am able to trim all Gimli's nails without any problems. It is a welcome pleasure for both dog and owner if this regular, and necessary, procedure can be performed without fear and panic.

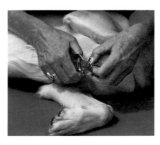

The Tail TTouch
Reduces fear and aggression

With Tail Work and the Tail TTouches, you can help your dog overcome fear and timidity (including fright from loud noises, such as thunder). This work can also be helpful with dogs that are aggressive toward other dogs, or "fear biters." The Tail TTouch eases pain and furthers recovery after injury or surgery (in addition, of course, to vet care), particularly with dogs that have problems getting up. It helps dogs regain their mobility; small, gentle circles, and very soft tail pulls can greatly improve the lives of dogs with hip dysplasia. They ease stiffness, which helps dogs lie down and get up.

WHAT IT LOOKS LIKE

Robyn starts doing the Tail TTouch on Shawnee who is lying on the ground. She stabilizes the body with her left hand while holding the tail lightly with her right hand. She is pulling the tail very gently and carefully in order to make a connection through the whole body.

Here, I am demonstrating the Tail Circle on Gimli. I lift the tail near its base with my right hand and move it around in a circle, rotating it in both directions. I am using my other hand to stabilize Gimli on his left haunch.

WHAT YOU SHOULD DO IF...

...the dog's docked tail is rigid and immobile

The TTouches are especially beneficial for animals with docked tails. The tails of some of these dogs are very stiff because they still retain the cellular memory of fear and pain from the docking surgery. In a case like this I recommend going over every square inch of the tail with small Raccoon TTouches. Pay special attention to the stump in order to remove any phantom pain. Move the tail in tiny circles. If you can loosen up a tight tail, your dog's range of motion and resulting self-confidence will greatly increase.

I am doing some Raccoon TTouches on Bandit's docked tail while stabilizing him with my hand under his belly. Some dogs have "phantom limb" pain in their docked tails, which can be alleviated with the Tail TTouches.

HOW TO

The way a dog carries his tail has many different meanings. If a dog is wagging his tail in a relaxed manner, he is, of course, expressing joy and a good mood. However, a nervous, hyperactive, or insecure dog may wag his tail constantly and very fast. When a dog holds his tail in a stiff, still, and high position, he is indicating dominance or aggression, while a dog that carries his tail between his legs is demonstrating fear and submission. Whatever the position of the tail, you can influence your dog's behavior by changing the way he carries it.

There are three ways to work on the tail:
1) A gentle pull and release will give the dog a feeling of connection. With the dog standing, or lying down, hold the tail at the root with one hand while supporting his body with your other hand. Pull gently and carefully, hold for a few seconds, then slowly release the tail.
2) Circling the tail in both directions releases both physical and emotional tension.
3) Raccoon TTouches on the tail allow a dog to let go of fear – acute, chronic, or longstanding fear.

The Leading Exercises

Why Do Them?

The Tellington TTouch leading methods offer many advantages to training, and are helpful for dogs that are disobedient, timid, and aggressive. With the Leading Exercises such dogs can learn to cooperate willingly and obey, even when off the leash.

One of the major problems a dog owner encounters is the dog that pulls on the leash. When the leash is constantly taut the dog learns to pull more because pressure produces counter pressure. In the long run, this habit can cause damage to the dog's larynx, neck, shoulders, pelvis, and back. Moreover, pulling strains the dog's back legs unnecessarily, and can cause hip or knee injuries as well. Many owners ignore this problem in small dogs because they pull with less force and are less difficult to hold than big dogs. However, small dogs sustain bodily injuries just as easily as big dogs. The Leading Exercises offer several solutions to these "pulling" habits.

There are several pieces of equipment we use for training, and retraining, a dog: the Halti in combination with a flat collar, the Body Wrap, the Double Diamond, and others are all helpful. They will be explained and demonstrated on the following pages.

We also use the "Wand" – an unusual aid for dog training. As I mentioned earlier, the Wand can be used in place of your hand with a dog that is concerned about being TTouched.

The Equipment

The following is a list of the special Tellington TTouch Method training equipment:

- **Flat Collar**: This is the basic Tellington TTouch tool for every dog and can be used in combination with the Halti. We use the flat collar in place of a choke chain, choke rope, or pinch (prong) collar.
- **Dog Harness**: A chest harness for dogs
- **Halti**: A head collar for dogs
- **Snoot Loop**: Very similar to the Halti, but more appropriate for dogs with a short muzzle.
- **Leash with Two Snaps**: This leash should be about 6 feet (2 m) long with two snaps – one stronger, and one lighter. (If you have difficulty finding a double-snapped leash, you can order one from

The Wand serves as an extension of the arm.

the TTouch Training office).
• **Body Wrap**: This consists of one or two elastic bandages, 3 inches (7 to 8 cm) wide by approximately 6 feet (2 m) long. Bandages are available in all sizes – choose one suitable for your dog.
• **The Wand**: A 3 foot (approx.1 m) long, stiff horse whip.

Safety First

• A Golden Rule: Keep the exercises short so that your dog has enough time to process what he has learned, and not get stressed by too much input.
• Always be especially careful if you are working with a strange, fearful, or aggressive dog.
• Do not stare a strange, nervous, or aggressive dog in the eyes. Many dogs experience this as a threat. If you are greeting a dog, or want to put on a Halti or a Body Wrap, it is safest to approach the dog from the side.

The Double Diamond, made of a smooth nylon rope, is most effective when used on dogs that spin, lunge, "flip-out," or are aggressive.

Leading a dog between two handlers improves his focus, balance, and attention.

The Balance Leash

An aid for correcting leash pullers

You can correct your dog's bad habit of pulling all the time by arranging your regular leash in a position across the dog's lower chest. We call this the Balance Leash. Using it, you shift your dog's center of gravity back. When this happens, the dog gets back into balance and begins to respond to your signals. When he learns not to pull, he can go back to wearing the leash in the usual way.

WHAT IT LOOKS LIKE

I am demonstrating how to lead a dog with the Balance Leash. I'm holding the leash with both hands as I walk next to Tess close to her head. I control the walking speed by lifting, or relaxing, the leash.

HOW TO

The leash should be at least 6 feet (2 m) long. Attach the leash to the dog's collar as usual, and sling it around your dog's chest. Hold the loop of the leash with one hand and the end of the leash with the other (see drawing). To slow down or stop, rebalance your dog with several very quick "pulls and releases." This helps the dog shift his weight back. Make sure that the end of the leash that is attached to the collar remains loose. With small dogs it is sometimes difficult to keep the leash on the chest because they have a tendency to step over the loop. In these cases we recommend using a harness, or a Halti, when they pull. With larger breeds this particular problem usually does not occur unless a dog spins or lunges. Make sure you walk normally when you are leading with a Balance Leash.

Using the Wand
Reduces fear

You can calm down a nervous dog by touching him all over with the Wand. Stroking the dog's legs from elbows and pelvis to the paws will give him a feeling of stability and grounding.

HOW TO

Using the Wand and, for safety, keeping your distance at about three feet, you can stroke the whole body of a nervous, or over sensitive, dog. The best way to use the Wand is to integrate it into the Leading Exercises. Start by stroking your dog on the areas of his body that you know he enjoys having TTouched until he begins to trust you. For a dog that chews on everything, and does not like to have his mouth touched, it is helpful to roll the button (knob) end of the Wand along the tongue and palate. This way the dog cannot chew on the Wand. This works for puppies in the teething phase, too.(Rolling the wand under the upper lip is a safe way to introduce the Mouth Work to a nervous, or resistant animal – as shown above.)

You can also use the Wand when playing with your puppy. When following the Wand around, a puppy is being prepared to be lead on a leash (and it's good exercise for him, too!). This will prepare him to be touched all over with the Wand, and then the hand.

WHAT IT LOOKS LIKE

Ever since being hit by a car, Jesse gets nervous when touched on the tail. By lifting her tail with the Wand, Kirsten alters her fear response and consequently, her behavior.

Cumae is a young, hyperactive dog. Stroking her back legs with a Wand helps to calm, and ground her.

Introducing the Halti
Preparation for the Leading Exercises

If your dog is young, hyperactive, unfocused, disobedient, aggressive toward other dogs, or pulls on the leash, you should use the Halti (a halter for dogs) for the Leading Exercises. We use it in combination with a flat collar. The advantage of using the Halti is that you can control your dog with a lot less force than just using a normal collar. Also, you can easily turn your dog's head to get his attention.

WHAT IT LOOKS LIKE

First, in order to prepare your dog for the contact and "confinement" of the Halti, do TTouches around his mouth and cover his muzzle with your hands. Then, as Robyn is doing here to Shawnee, place a piece of elastic loosely around the dog's muzzle at the same time talking in a calm voice.

Next, Robyn crosses this piece of elastic under Shawnee's mouth, takes both ends to the back of the neck, and makes a simple knot. As soon as Shawnee is comfortable with this "practice" Halti, the next step follows.

Robyn is showing Shawnee a real Halti in order to prepare her for wearing it. Before you put a Halti on your dog's head, please look at it carefully so that there is no unnecessary confusion and fumbling as you fit it.

WHAT YOU SHOULD DO...

...to check that the Halti is comfortable

The Halti should be loose enough so that you can slip both your thumbs into the top of the cheek straps. Make sure that the nose strap does not slide off. If this happens, try a short-nose Halti, or a Snoot Loop. A Snoot Loop is constructed like the Halti but it stays on the head more securely because of the extra strap along the forehead.

Robyn places the Halti over the elastic and closes the snap at the dog's neck. She combines the elastic with the Halti in order to get Shawnee to accept the Halti quickly and easily. Your dog should wear the Halti for a while without a leash attached to it.

The leash should be light and about 6-to-8 feet long. Attach one end to the flat collar, and the other one to the bottom ring of the Halti. Hold the leash in both hands.

If you don't have a piece of elastic to prepare the dog for the Halti, you can also put the leash around his muzzle as shown in this photo. Lightly hold it there until the dog accepts it. With some dogs it is important to be patient but calmly insistent.

Leading with the Halti
Promotes successful leading

Leading a dog with a Halti may be a somewhat unusual experience in the beginning. We recommend you hold the leash, which is attached to the Halti and the collar, with both hands. After you have practiced it for some time, however, you will notice how simple and comfortable it is, and how much easier it is to control your dog.

WHAT IT LOOKS LIKE

This is the "neutral" position: if you are standing on the right side of your dog your right hand holds the end of the leash attached to the Halti while your left hand holds the end attached to the collar. Both parts of the leash should be as loose as possible. Position yourself next to your dog's head. To ensure that your contact is light enough, place your thumbs forward along the leash.

To ask your dog to start *walking*, gently tug at the part of the leash that is attached to the collar and release it immediately. Do not expect your dog to start walking when you tug – the *release* is the signal to move. Your verbal signals are important as well. Combine your movement on the leash with a "Let's go!"

If you want to *turn* your dog *in your direction* gently pull the part of the leash that is attached to the Halti. You should announce all turns with a quiet signal on the Halti, and most dogs will react correctly. However, if your dog does not turn from this Halti signal, give him a gentle pull on his collar as well.

HOW TO

Halti Training is a very helpful way of teaching your dog to respond to light signals, and not to pull. When leading your dog with both hands, be very conscious of which part of the leash you use first. For example, if you want to start walking, give your first signal on the collar. If you want to turn your dog give the first signal on the Halti. Many people habitually hold the leash tight, and clench their fists, even when their dogs are not moving at all. Practice keeping a slack leash at all times when your dog is not moving. Your dog should stand in self-balance and not support himself on a "fifth leg" (the leash), because pulling always leads to more pulling. You can change your dog's bad habit of pulling on the leash by changing your own bad leading habits as well.

If you want to **turn** the dog *away from you* place the part of the leash that is attached to the Halti against his muzzle and point the dog's head in the required direction.

WHAT YOU SHOULD DO IF...

...the dog tries to get the Halti off

If you use a piece of elastic to get your dog prepared for the Halti this problem should not occur. However, there are dogs that are oversensitive to anything near their muzzle that have a hard time accepting the Halti. In these cases allow the dogs to wear the Halti without the leash attached. Also, lift the dog's head when he tries to paw it off. Be patient and check to be sure the strap under the jaw isn't too tight. Stay calm, be consistent, and keep the exercises short. Among all the dogs we have worked with there were only two who would not wear a Halti. Both those dogs had been previously abused, and obviously considered wearing the Halti a punishment.

The leash is attached to the Halti **and** to the collar.

Case History

Sarah, an exuberant Jack Russell/Pit Bull Cross

Peg Ebata writes:

" Sunday, August 29 has been designated as Sarah's birthday. It was the day Sarah and I witnessed the miracle of the TTouches. Sarah, a rambunctious Jack Russell/Pit Bull cross, while grunting like a pig, dragged me into a Tellington TTouch clinic, and then refused to sit still while introductions were being made. It was not an auspicious beginning!

When it was time to begin work with the animals, Linda Tellington-Jones looked directly at us, and asked, "Would Sarah like to come up first?" Sarah lunged to the front of the class. Linda fit her with a Halti, wrapped a climbing rope securely around her body, and told us that Sarah's furiously wagging tail signaled fear and insecurity, rather than joy. She began doing TTouches on Sarah's body –steady, circular movements that calmed her – and instructed me to hold her tail still while I did TTouches on her tail and back. As soon as Sarah's tail became still, it was possible for her to feel her body, concentrate, and absorb the healing work being done.

Shortly afterward, Linda was able to lead Sarah through a maze laid out on the floor, a task that would have been impossible before the TTouch work. We did TTouches on her while other dogs in the clinic went up for help, and she continued to wear the Halti and climbing rope brace for the entire day. But even by lunchtime, three hours later, she was significantly calmer, and lay on the floor to observe the other dogs. Workshop participants came up to say, "It's a miracle!" And it was. This experience has given Sarah and me a chance to heal our relationship, and I am deeply grateful to Linda for the work she does. Thank you. "

Case History

Nico, a German Shepherd – Aggressive

Cynthia D'Aquini writes:

Robyn and Shawnee demonstrate how to lead a dog with a Halti using both hands.

“ I own three German Shepherds – Max (our alpha dog) is eight years old; Contess is seven; and Nico is almost two. When Nico was a puppy he was bitten twice – by two different dogs. One was Max, who bit him on the face – though now, I'm glad to say, they get along. However, because of his bad experiences, Nico grew up not trusting any strange dogs – in fact he attacked them as soon as he saw them.

Nico usually behaved well at show trials but even there his aggression occasionally appeared in the ring. That is the reason why I decided to order Linda Tellington-Jones' books and try the techniques she described. I did Clouded Leopard TTouches and Ear TTouches in order to calm him down and to boost his confidence. By leading him with the Halti I was able to control him better and to help him negotiate the various obstacles.

It was really like a miracle! At our next competition everyone wanted to know who my new dog was – people just could not believe that this calm and relaxed dog was Nico. Since then he has been "Best of Breed" twice and has won other important titles as well.

Nico, and my other dogs, love their daily TTouches sessions in the evening. They really seem to look forward to them, and afterward they all sleep peacefully. ”

The Body Wrap
An aid for the leading exercises

The Body Wrap enhances your dog's sense of his own body and makes him more confident in his movements and behavior. It is especially beneficial for dogs that are afraid of loud noise, nervous, hyperactive, or panic when riding in a car. The Body Wrap also helps injured dogs to recover; moreover, it is helpful for older, stiff, and arthritic dogs. There are several versions of wrapping. Experiment to find out which type of Body Wrap is the most appropriate for your dog.

WHAT IT LOOKS LIKE

The Half Wrap is used mainly on dogs that are nervous about having their hindquarters wrapped, or on dogs who have knee or hip problems. Place the center of the bandage across the dog's chest, then cross the ends on the back and under the belly. Take both ends up to the back and secure them with a safety pin.

This Body Wrap is a continuation of the Half Wrap. Instead of fastening the ends of the bandage with a safety pin, cross them again over the back and take them through the inside of your dog's thighs. Then bring both ends (without crossing them again) to the top of the back, and secure them with a safety pin. For a big dog you will need two bandages.

HOW TO

This is the type of Body Wrap we use most frequently. It is easy to put on and very effective. Use elastic bandages for a Body Wrap. Place the middle of the bandage across the dog's chest and cross the ends once on the back. Then take both ends (without crossing them) between the back legs and back along the outside of the thighs. Sling the ends through the bandage on both sides of the body and connect them on the back. Make sure that the bandage stays as flat as possible. If it is too loose it will not be very effective. However, if the bandage is too tight it can interfere with your dog's movement and impair his circulation.

Here is another variation of the Body Wrap. Place the bandage around the dog's neck so that you have a long and a short end. Make a simple knot (or use a safety pin) over one of the shoulders. Then take the long end along the dog's back all the way to the tail. Pull the bandage from behind between the legs along the inside of one thigh, then across the back to the other side. Take the bandage from the front around the inside of the other hind leg and then along the back next to the tail. When you reach that part of the Wrap that runs across the back take your end and slip it under the Wrap, then take the end back to the shoulder and fasten it.

WHAT YOU SHOULD DO IF...

...the dog will not move, seems scared, or lies down wearing the Body Wrap

If your dog's hips or knees are sensitive it could be that a whole Body Wrap is too much for him. Instead, use a Half Wrap, which often helps to improve a dog's mobility. If your dog is scared you can prepare him for the Body Wrap with some TTouches on his hindquarters. Or, first use a Half Wrap to help your dog get used to the new sensation.

Doing groundwork with a Body Wrap helps a nervous dog become more confident.

Case History

Cody, an Australian Sheepdog – difficult to lead

Phyllis Bauerlein writes:

" When I saw Cody for the first time he was a lively, rambunctious puppy with a short attention span, and no manners. His owner, Wilma, was upset because, among doing other things that made life difficult, he constantly pulled on the leash and she was tired of jerking it to correct him. And, on the day before I met her she had been trying to trim Cody's nails but that had been impossible.

I tried some TTouches on him but it was difficult because he threw himself from side to side, wriggled, and tried to chew my hand. I put a Body Wrap on him, which became just another chew toy, until I got the Halti on and we went outside to practice leading. He responded instantly, started to concentrate, listened to me, and did not pull on the lead. After a few minutes, Wilma led him and he behaved nicely for her too. After about fifteen minutes he sat down quietly while we did TTouches on his body and his mouth.

We went back inside, Cody lay down next to Wilma. He was so relaxed that he did not move at all while we continued doing Clouded Leopard and Raccoon TTouches all over him. Wilma said that in all the time she had had Cody she had never been able to touch him for such a long time. Cody finally fell asleep and we stayed for a while to talk. When I got up to leave he woke up. I took his regular leash and had no problem leading him outside.

Two days later Wilma phoned to tell me that Cody had been behaving much better since our first meeting. He even stood quietly for her when she was drying his paws after a walk. She told me that I had performed a miracle. Of course that was very flattering, but the truth is that the change in Cody was due to The Tellington TTouch work. "

Case History

Sparky, a mixed breed – difficult to lead

Phyllis Bauerlein writes:

The Body Wrap can be put on in many different ways

" Tracy, the owner of a two-year-old Collie/Labrador mix, asked me for help. As a puppy, Sparky had been in several different obedience classes, but Tracy still had problems keeping him from pulling on the leash. In addition, Sparky was very over-enthusiastic, and jumped on people to greet them.

Very unhappily (because she did not want to have to use such a harsh training device because Sparky was a friendly dog that just lacked concentration), Tracy had even tried a "prong" collar to stop him pulling, but the problems had only become worse. My impression was that Sparky was confused by different training methods tried on him.

The Body Wrap and Halti changed Sparky's behavior entirely. She immediately stopped pulling on the leash, and became calm and focused. I also showed her several TTouches, such as the Clouded Leopard, the Lying Leopard, the Abalone, the Mouth and Ear TTouch. These TTouches helped to establish an even deeper connection between Tracy and her dog. "

The Double Diamond
A leading aid

The Double Diamond is a leading aid to help train aggressive dogs, and dogs that lunge or are out of control. In addition, dogs that refuse to walk on a leash, or simply lie down when asked to do so, can be helped by being led with the Double Diamond.

WHAT IT LOOKS LIKE

I am gently pulling the Double Diamond to the front, giving Tess a signal to walk faster. I recommend doing these exercises from both sides of the dog because this activates both sides of the brain. Moreover, it is healthier for the neck, shoulders, and legs of both dogs and humans.

HOW TO

Use a soft, smooth nylon rope that doesn't stretch (a nautical or climbing rope works well). I recommend doubling up the rope to increase the area of contact. The rope should be about 21 feet (7–8 m) long, and the diameter about $\frac{1}{4}$ inch ($\frac{1}{2}$ cm) for a small dog, and about $\frac{3}{8}$ inch (1 cm) for a larger dog.

Place the center of the doubled rope across the dog's chest, and cross the ends over the top of the shoulders. Pull the ends of the rope and cross them under the belly. Bring the ends over the dog's back, and tie the ends together a few inches higher than the back (above the back). Make another square knot so that the rope will stay on the back if you let go of it. If you want a loop to lead the dog you need to knot the ends of the rope together.

The Dog Harness
A leading aid

Some dog owners have great success in correcting leash pulling by using a harness. Other people, whose dogs walk nicely on the leash, use the harness because they consider it more humane than a collar. The harness is also a good alternative to a collar for a dog that has been injured by a choke chain. The harness can also be used in combination with a Halti.

HOW TO

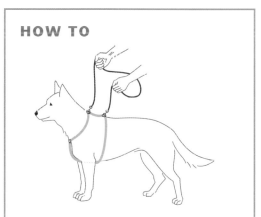

Dog harnesses come in different colors and sizes. We prefer a harness that has two rings on the upper strap – the one that runs along the spine. By attaching your dog this way you can prevent him from pulling, as well as give more effective directional signals. Many dogs will walk in a zigzag fashion if you attach the leash to the rear ring or front ring only, because they are not receiving clear signals. For a dog that is over-energetic, cannot concentrate, or pulls on the leash, it is useful to use both hands by attaching the ends of the leash to both rings (as in this drawing).

WHAT IT LOOKS LIKE

When leading a dog with both hands hold the leashes loosely running them between your thumbs and index fingers. This enables you to give small, subtle, and effective signals. Hold your hands parallel at a height that is comfortable for you. Here I am walking a little bit behind Tess, and my hands are parallel to the dog's body. In this position I can give Tess signals to turn, stop, or speed-up at any time.

The Journey of the Homing Pigeon

A leading exercise using two people

The Journey of the Homing Pigeon is a technique for leading animals from both sides. I have been using it for many years to guide and control difficult horses. This method is just as effective with dogs. Nervous animals gain confidence because they are given a clear direction, and are not able to charge ahead. In addition, some dogs feel protected by having people on both sides of them. This leading position is particularly effective for working with overactive, unfocused dogs.

WHAT IT LOOKS LIKE

WITH A WAND
Robyn and I are using the Journey of the Homing Pigeon in the neutral position – both leashes are loose. Note that the leashes are attached on opposite sides of the collar. I am showing Shawnee the direction with the Wand, and she is walking along attentively.

ACROSS THE POLES
Robyn and I are walking across the obstacle with Shawnee because she is still insecure. The goal is to get Shawnee to concentrate on negotiating the obstacle while getting used to having me close to her.

WHAT YOU SHOULD DO IF...

...you do not have a Wand, or feel unsure about using one

You can use a stick, or any other similar device. If your dog has been abused with a stick just give the signals with the leashes, your voice, and hand signals. You can certainly do this training without a Wand. However, a Wand is a useful aid once you've practiced.

IN THE LABYRINTH

Shawnee still seems unsure about being led from both sides. I am stroking her with the Wand to build a connection with her. Robyn is asking her to walk around the corner by giving her a signal on the Halti. Since Shawnee does not react to the first signal on the Halti, Robyn reinforces it with an additional signal on the collar.

HOW TO

When you lead a dog from both sides you need two leashes, a flat collar, a Halti, and a Wand. Attach both leashes to the collar and attach one of them to the Halti. There should be a space between the attachments of the two leashes on the collar so that you do not give signals on the same spot. This is confusing to the dog. The two people should walk at the head of the dog at a distance of about three feet out to the side. They should coordinate their signals. The signals for start, stop, and turn should be given clearly. To achieve smooth cooperation it is best if one person acts as the primary leader giving the signal, with the other person reinforcing it. It's a good idea in most instances for the dog's owner to be one of the people leading; two strangers should lead only if the dog is comfortable with them. Dogs who are aggressive toward other dogs can be controlled very safely in the Homing Pigeon. However, we do not recommend working with dogs that are aggressive toward people. Leave that to an experienced dog trainer who uses positive reinforcement, or call one of our dog practitioners who specialize in aggressive dogs.

Case History

Kong, a Dachshund who resisted in the show ring

Kathryn Lehman writes:

" Kong is a longhaired standard Dachshund conformation champion and show dog. He is a really handsome fellow with great potential to win at the shows. When Kong began to have issue with going into the show ring and allowing the judge to approach him, his owners decided to try the Tellington TTouch with him.

Since Kong was entered in upcoming shows and there was no TTouch clinic nearby, he came to me for a week of TTouch work. The first night was a disaster. He barked hysterically, and chased my husband, Terry, around the house acting as if he was going to bite him. I kept doing TTouches on him especially around his hindquarters as that area felt like a rock. He calmed a bit, but still got excited if Terry even moved.

It is important to keep in mind what a breed is bred to do. Dachshunds are bred to go into holes and kill badgers. A dog like this must be very brave and may not be naturally very friendly with strangers. Our goal is to help him do his "job" and be happy and calm in his work.

Kong's TTouch sessions varied in length. At first, I did a quick evaluation by gently moving my hands over his entire body. He did not seem to have any sore areas, but his hindquarters were very tight. I did Clouded Leopard TTouches all over his body with emphasis on his hindquarters. I worked with him for about four sessions of 20 minutes each. I did some light work around his mouth at the beginning. The last session of the evening I did about 5 minutes of actual Mouth work, including "playing the piano" on the back of his tongue area.

The next night, I put a Body Wrap on him. As soon as he

Leading a dog from both sides...

Case History cont.

got his body wrap on, it was one of those Magic TTouch moments! He calmed, stopped all barking and running around. He climbed up into my lap and laid his head on my chest. We were all very surprised. As he lay in my lap, I did more Clouded Leopard on his body. His hindquarters had softened at this point, but I still gave that area special attention with about 5 minutes of Raccoon TTouches.

His owners came to get him and they were really surprised. They brought their son and daughter-in-law along. Kong did not know their son at all. Bruce reported that generally Kong would have barked at new people, but he just stood calmly with my dogs and greeted them. The real test was he went to a dog show last weekend and showed better than he ever had – he was totally relaxed. Big surprise here! He was totally relaxed. Bruce could not believe it and is looking forward to continuing Kong's show career and using the TTouch to help Kong become the winner he has the potential to be. 〞

...helps to enhance concentration and coordination.

The Confidence Course

Why Do It?

Dogs enjoy working in the Confidence Course. You have probably watched dogs enthusiastically competing in an agility course – flying over jumps, rushing through a tunnel, whipping round the slalom course, and having a great time. In the Tellington TTouch Method, we work with obstacles, not for agility competition, but to develop awareness and confidence. We find we can develop a dog's willingness to focus and listen, to wait for our signals, and to overcome aggression or timidity. Your dog learns how to think and cooperate, because he has to concentrate on a given task. And, we teach dogs that take part in agility competitions, to slow down over obstacles in the beginning because this actually makes them faster and more precise in competition.

Physically, this training makes your dog more agile, supple, and balanced. The sense of achievement is, of course, equally impor-tant. If you praise your dog for each small step on the way to every exercise he masters, you will increase his self-confidence enormously.

Working a dog through the Labyrinth is an important part of Tellington TTouch training. Human studies have shown, among other things, that the work in the Labyrinth improves mobility and coordination in children with physical and learning disabilities. Our work with dogs (and horses, too) shows that attentiveness, coordination, cooperation, and balance are increased noticeably.

Leading a dog over various surfaces – boards, wire screens, and plastic sheets for example, helps to prepare him for situations where he has to walk across unusual surfaces, such as a smooth wood floor in a house, or a metal grate in the street.

Training with other obstacles such as Poles, the Star, Cavaletti, Tires, the Ladder, Cones, and the Teeter-Totter (see-saw) help to get your dog focused, and are fun for him, too.

The Labyrinth.

The Obstacles

• **6 poles**: For the Labyrinth, plastic poles are best. They should be 10 to 12 feet (2 to 3.5 m) long, and their diameter should be $1\frac{1}{2}$ to 3 inches (4 to 8 cm) You can use shorter plastic pipes – approx. 3 feet (1 m) long – and assemble them or join them with "sleeves" or connectors. These shorter pieces are easier to store. You can use the same poles for the training the dog with the Poles, the Star, and the Cavaletti.

• **A board**: It should be about 8 feet (2.5 m) long, 1 foot (30 cm) wide, and 1 inch (approx. 2 cm) thick. With a round wooden block underneath, it can be turned into the Teeter-Totter (see-saw). With tires, plastic, or wooden blocks it becomes the Board Walk.

• **A plastic sheet and a wire mesh sheet**: These are used to expose a dog to various surfaces. Sheets of 3 feet by 6 feet (1 m by 2 m) are appropriate.

• **6 tires**: You can place the tires either close together, or with spaces in between, depending on how well your dog handles these obstacles.

• **A ladder**: Use a regular ladder made of wood or aluminum.

• **6 cones**: Cones can be used to set up a slalom for a dog to run through. But poles, and other objects, can also be used to mark out a course.

Make agility obstacles as easy as possible in the beginning and, in order to help him learn, ask your dog to walk slowly over them. You can always have him speed up later on.

Working through cavaletti improve's a dog's gait and mobility.

Safety Tips

• It is important that all obstacles are constructed safely. Watch out for movable parts, sharp edges, and splinters.

• Be careful when working with a dog that is aggressive toward other dogs. Keep a sufficient distance.

• Lead a difficult dog in the Homing Pigeon position (with another person). He will be easier to control and consequently learn faster.

Small dogs can learn to negotiate big obstacles.

The Labyrinth
Trains concentration

The Labyrinth is one the exercises we use the most. Focus, coordination, concentration, obedience, and balance, are all markedly increased when dogs work through this obstacle. Because of the boundaries indicated by the poles, your dog learns to concentrate on you and pay attention to the subtle signals you give on the leash, with your voice, or with your body language.

WHAT IT LOOKS LIKE

Shawnee needs to get used to the new experience of wearing a Halti so is being led through the Labyrinth in order to divert her attention from it. Robyn is turned toward Shawnee so she can watch her and control her speed by lifting and releasing the leash. Robyn also indicates the direction of movement by turning her right arm and her upper body. As Shawnee is doing, your dog should walk in the center between the poles of the Labyrinth.

From this front view you can see that Robyn's hands are at different levels. Note the distance between dog and handler, and that both ends of the leash are loose. Again, Robyn has turned her upper body toward Shawnee to watch her and control her speed.

HOW TO

Walking an aggressive, or nervous dog through the Labyrinth with another calmer dog (or dogs) is a good exercise. It doesn't matter if the other dog goes first, or follows your dog. If you are working with a "dog-aggressive" dog, make sure that you keep a sufficient distance from other dogs when passing them.

These photos demonstrate that Shawnee is able to be close to Tess and remain calm after just one exercise. However, in order to eliminate aggression completely it will be necessary to work frequently – not only with one new dog, but with other strange dogs, too. Through this non-habitual exercise – working an aggressive dog with a quiet one – it is possible to change the aggressive dog's behavior completely. The Labyrinth gives the dog a new boundary that helps him to change his habitual behavior pattern.

1. Shawnee lunges at Tess as the two dogs are led through the Labyrinth. Robyn is turning Shawnee's head with the Halti and is pulling Shawnee toward her with the leash that is attached to the collar.

2. This time Robyn places herself between the dogs. Shawnee is watching Tess nervously, and is ready to attack. The Halti with the double leash helps Robyn control Shawnee.

3. After several practice runs, I stay in one place with Tess while Robyn walks toward us. Note that both Robyn and I are positioned between the dogs.

4. Robyn allows Shawnee to look in Tess' direction as long as Shawnee stays calm. At the same time, I stroke Shawnee with a Wand to calm her and establish contact.

The Platform and Boards

For trust and confidence

The first exercise, the Platform, is raised on tires with poles on the sides for a focal boundary. The width of the Platform is not standard but should be wide enough to give a dog confidence initially. The second, the Boards, is comprised of two boards, 1 foot (30 cm) wide by 8 feet (2.4 m) long. Work over both these obstacles develops physical, mental, and emotional balance, and aids concentration and focus.

Setting the platform on tires is useful for dogs that become nervous in unfamiliar situations, such as slippery or unusual footing, or when climbing an open flight of stairs. Working with the narrower boards flat on the ground is often more challenging to a dog's balance. It is the first step toward advanced work on raised boards used in agility courses.

WHAT IT LOOKS LIKE

T-Rex is a young dog that concentrates better when he is lead from both sides. Here Kirsten and I stop him before he steps the whole way on to the platform. We do this so that he will learn to slow down and think before he acts.

T-Rex walks quietly over the platform following the Wand, with the leashes slightly loose in "neutral." Notice that my leash is attached to the collar on the opposite side from Kirsten's. If both leashes were attached to the same ring the dog would receive confusing signals.

WHAT YOU SHOULD DO IF...

...the dog is unfocused and not paying attention

Be mindful of your own focus and concentration. Pause for a few seconds before the obstacle, and have a clear picture in your mind of what you want your dog to do. Then proceed over the boards, being sure to reward him for small steps using your voice and doing a few quiet Circular TTouches on his shoulder.

Work on a single board like this can profoundly influence a dog's physical and emotional balance. We use the second board in the beginning until a dog is confident, attentive, and sure-footed enough to walk over a single one. To raise the obstacle and make a Board Walk, you can place tires, or plastic and wooden blocks underneath.

Here we use two narrower boards close together to see how Tess maneuvers on them without any pole boundaries. My goal is to get her to walk on just one board. Notice how she starts off on the one board, but steps on the second one for balance, and she is not focusing on the Wand.

The boards are spread further apart at one end to get Tess' attention and let her see the distinct edges of the boards as boundaries. She begins to concentrate on the movement of the Wand.

Success – Tess has the idea now. She follows the Wand and can balance easily on a single board. She's ready for the next step, which is to raise both ends, either on tires or cement blocks.

Wire Mesh and Plastic Surfaces
For balance and confidence

Leading your dog over a wire mesh screen, or a plastic surface, is a good way to train him to follow you onto any unusual or slippery surfaces. It is also an important exercise in the training of Therapy Dogs and Search-and-Rescue Dogs who have to walk securely, and without fear, on any surface. For an unusual surface, use fine gauge window screen material and staple it to a frame. Any kind of hard plastic that does not splinter can be used to simulate an icy surface.

WHAT IT LOOKS LIKE

I am using an ordinary leash on Jesse for the first time over the fine wire screen attached to a thick frame. Jesse is walking slowly and placing her feet carefully. I am encouraging her with my voice and praising her for successfully trying to negotiate the obstacle.

Young dogs learn more quickly being led from both sides over an obstacle. Using both hands Kirsten is leading T-Rex with a lead attached to both the collar and a Halti, while I am further away and just using a regular leash attached to the collar, and a Wand. The leashes are in a neutral position so that the dog is free to investigate the surface.

HOW TO

If your dog gets nervous when working with obstacles and clenches his paws, we recommend preparing him with Raccoon TTouches on the paws. This way you can get his attention as well as build a new connection to his paws. If a dog is frightened, his muscles get tense and this restricts the circulation in the legs all the way down. As a result his paws become numb. In addition, you can put a Body Wrap on him in order to give him more security and stability. You can also encourage the dog by placing some food on the obstacle. The more unusual walking surfaces you can offer your dog, the more trusting and self-confident he will be in all new situations.

Using both hands, Jo is leading Gimli over a slippery plastic surface. Gimli, with his nose on the ground, is concentrating and is placing his feet carefully.

WHAT YOU SHOULD DO IF...

...you don't have access to an agility course

The obstacles that we use are as simple as possible. You can make them from materials that you already have around the house. You really do not need a professional training course with agility obstacles. Tellington TTouch obstacles can be set up quickly in your backyard, or in a parking lot. You can use an ordinary large sheet of plastic to simulate a slippery surface, and mesh window screen for the wire surface.

The Teeter-Totter (See-Saw)

For self-assurance and confidence

The Teeter-Totter (See-Saw) is an obstacle that is especially suitable for improving your dog's balance and sure footedness. He will learn to trust you in any situation, even in an unexpected situation. You can vary the degree of difficulty by changing the height of the Teeter-Totter.

WHAT IT LOOKS LIKE

Stop in front of the Teeter-Totter and lightly tap the board with your Wand to call your dog's attention to the obstacle. Gimli is following Jo's Wand as she walks next to Gimli's head.

Using the Wand, Jo thwarts Gimli's attempt to get off the board before finishing the exercise. This mistake occurred because Jo is standing too far back and forgot that Gimli is supposed to follow the Wand.

WHAT YOU SHOULD DO IF...

...the dog jumps off the teeter-totter

Simplify the obstacle. Use a wide board and a smaller block. Put some food on the board to encourage your dog to walk slowly. Take your time and proceed slowly, step-by-step. If your dog jumps off, or does not walk in a straight line, try using a Halti and, perhaps, a Double Diamond. Make sure you stay at the dog's head when leading him.

HOW TO

1. Jesse walked along this board on the ground before it was put on the tire to make a teeter-totter. Now, she is watching as a helper puts some food on the obstacle to encourage her to walk on it again.

2. I balance the board on the tire so that one end cannot tip. I lead Jesse with a rope that I've placed around her chest, right behind her shoulder. This helps me to control direction.

3. I stop Jesse as the board tips down. I am supporting her by her collar and the chest ring, so that she waits calmly.

4. We raise the Teeter-Totter to make it lighter. I am putting my weight on the board to tip it down slowly while Jesse stands in the middle getting used to the motion.

The A-Frame, and the Board Walk
Fun with agility training

The A-Frame and the Board Walk are obstacles that are also used in agility training. Apart from the fun you and your dog will have, these exercises improve your dog's agility, balance, and self-confidence. The A-Frame consists of two boards attached together with a hinge and a chain underneath. Slats prevent your dog from sliding. The angle of the incline should be adjustable – make the slope easy to begin. An elevated board, the Board Walk (with a pole on either side here) is used to give a dog confidence to negotiate the Teeter-Totter, the A-Frame, and the raised Board Walk.

WHAT IT LOOKS LIKE

ASCENDING THE A-FRAME
Here the A-Frame is set lower than it would be for agility training so that Jesse can get used to it. I am helping Jesse up with the Wand, and she is following calmly and slowly.

DESCENDING THE A-FRAME
For some dogs the descent is more difficult than the ascent. Jesse is trying to find her correct balance and is placing her foot slowly and carefully. I am walking a little bit ahead of her and she is following me willingly.

WHAT YOU SHOULD DO IF...

...the dog has hip problems

Avoid work on the A-Frame because the slope can cause pain. Be aware that climbing stairs and jumping into a car can exacerbate hip problems, so limit these and other athletic activities.

HOW TO

Agility training with a steep A-Frame and a raised Board Walk is for more advanced dogs. Here, I am showing some simpler variations that can lead to unexpected success with nervous and insecure dogs. Because these exercises are challenging, the animals gain new experiences that increase their self-assurance and confidence. If your dog is too fast, use a Halti in combination with a collar for this training. You should also have a very clear idea of how much you can ask your dog to do depending on his health, age, and breed. For safety, dogs with hip dysplasia, or arthritis, should not be asked to walk over the A-Frame or raised Board Walk. The goal of these exercises is for your dog to negotiate the obstacles slowly and carefully. Therefore, you should slow down your dog if he rushes.

THE BOARD WALK

Since Jesse at first hesitated to walk on this board, I placed poles on either side. This helped Jesse walk confidently and in a straight line. This is important for the next step of raising the board.

Cavaletti, The Star, and Poles
More fun with agility training

Exercises with Cavaletti, The Star, and Poles will improve your dog's concentration, focus, and agility. He learns to move with awareness. Poles are also good training for improving the gait and fitness of show dogs, and for preparing dogs for agility classes. Light plastic poles are best, and can easily be transformed into Cavaletti and the Star. You need 5 or 6 poles, 3 to 6 feet (1 to 2 m) long.

WHAT IT LOOKS LIKE

CAVALETTI

Jo is leading Gimli over 6 cavaletti. Gimli jogs over the center of the poles while Jo walks next to the cavaletti showing Gimli the way with her Wand. This exercise is used to improve a dog's gait and lightness of movement.

THE STAR

Gimli is following Jo's Wand through The Star, which here, consists of 6 poles. Gimli is walking on the inside, which is more difficult than the outside, because the poles are higher and closer together. This is a great exercise for improving general coordination.

HOW TO

1. Experiment to find out which distance between the poles is most comfortable for your dog at the trot. Pay attention to your balance and how you step over the poles as well – your body language will motivate and influence him.

2. Here, the last pole has been raised. The poles before the jump help Jesse judge the distance and stay in rhythm.

WHAT YOU SHOULD DO IF...

...the dog participates but with no enjoyment

Make sure you praise your dog for each success. If you are enjoying yourself and are having fun, your dog will probably feel the same. Also, consider inviting friends and their dogs so that you can all work together. Making the training a social event will probably motivate both you and your dog.

3. I jump next to Jesse over the pole, which is raised to about 16 inches (40 cm). Jesse and I are moving in perfect sync and we are obviously having a lot of fun.

The Ladder and The Tires
Even more fun with obstacles

The Ladder and The Tires exercises are a challenge for some dogs. The different materials and shapes of these objects provide new experiences. Each exercise influences a dog in a way that cannot be predicted. For The Ladder exercise, put a simple ladder on the ground. For The Tires, use 4 to 8 tires, and place them in various configurations. The object is to create challenges that will develop a dog's confidence in dealing with new, and unusual, situations.

WHAT IT LOOKS LIKE

I am leading Tess over The Ladder with an ordinary leash and a Wand. Tess steps carefully into the spaces between the rungs following the Wand closely.

Uta and I are demonstrating how to steady Jesse who wants to walk quickly over the tires because she feels insecure. The Homing Pigeon position, using the Halti with the double leash, gives her more security and enhances her confidence.

Grady, a two-year-old Standard Poodle is being led over an obstacle for the first time. Stroking him with the Wand on his front legs helps him to calm down so that he can concentrate on the obstacle. Robyn is leading him with a Balance Leash in order to bring him into balance and to stop him from forging ahead. Since Grady is nervous about walking on, or even touching, The Tires, they have been placed in such a way that there is a space between the rows. This simplifies the obstacle. The goal is for the dog to be successful, so make the obstacles easy in the beginning, working up to more difficult challenges. In this way, we can start him off walking between the tires. The objective is to get the dog to walk along the rims, and then into the middle of the tires themselves.

HOW TO

When working with The Ladder your dog has to pay close attention to what he is doing, and adjust the length of his stride to the distance between the rungs. If your dog is afraid, and will not step into the spaces between the rungs you zigzag him back and forth across The Ladder several times, follow another dog, or put some treats in the spaces between the rungs. If you want to help your dog walk the entire length, and he is somewhat insecure, you can place one side of the ladder next to a wall. This way you only need to control your dog on one side and he cannot step out of The Ladder.

When working with The Tires, your dog can start by walking on the rims. Increase the difficulty by asking him to step into the center of the tires. Some dogs will be encouraged if you drop treats into the middle of The Tires.

WHAT YOU SHOULD DO IF...

...the dog keeps stepping off the obstacle

One idea is to put a visual boundary next to The Ladder, or The Tires, using plain or multi-colored poles. Poles are also useful as a sort of signpost in front of an obstacle. You can place them in the form of a V so they show the dog the way to the start of the exercise. If your dog steps off an obstacle, just lead him back to it and try again. You may also have to try a simpler obstacle first or make the present one easier. Make sure that you let your dog advance slowly, step-by-step, and that you stay forward, near his head. Remember to praise him a lot with your voice and with TTouches. If you are working with a shy or nervous dog, it is a good idea to have treats in your pocket.

The Slalom with Cones

Flexibility exercise

Focus and flexibility are emphasized in the Slalom made up of cones. This is another obstacle that you may know from regular dog agility training. It is great fun for both dogs and humans. At first, practice the slalom with a leash, and at slow speed. Once your dog understands what he is supposed to do, you can speed up, and finally even discard the leash. You need 5 to 6 cones set up in a straight line. When you start, the distance between the cones should be at least $1\frac{1}{2}$ times as long as the dog's body.

WHAT IT LOOKS LIKE

Tess is running through the cones without a leash. I am directing her with hand signals and body language. She is cooperating well and is running in tight curves around the cones while watching my right hand. Sometimes, you may find it helpful to use treats to motivate a dog to do this exercise.

If you keep your training sessions short you will find that your dog processes what he has learned between sessions, and will be more skilled the next time.

WHAT YOU SHOULD DO IF...

...the dog skips a cone

Increase the space between the cones because the dog may be finding tight turns difficult. If so, check to see if the dog has a physical problem that makes turning hard for him. If not, it could be lack of flexibility or focus. It can also be helpful to follow another team through the cones, and also do some TTouches to increase mobility and balance.

HOW TO

1. Shawnee is wearing a Halti and a Body Wrap to gain confidence. Robyn is using both hands on the leash to guide Shawnee through the cones.

2. Robyn's clear signals on the leash emphasize the turn. Shawnee must learn to stay as close to the cones as possible in order to negotiate the cones smoothly and quickly.

3. Concentration is important for the Slalom. Practice running the Slalom course in both directions, and lead the dog from both sides. As a result, both of you will become more flexible.

TTouch Training Plan for Your Dog

Name: _____ Age: _____ Breed: _____

Jot down in the chart how your dog reacts to the TTouches, the Leading Exercises, and the Confidence Course. Use a scale from 1 to 5: 1 = no acceptance; 5 = optimal acceptance.

TTOUCHES	DATE	DATE	DATE	DATE	DATE	DATE
Clouded Leopard TTouch						
Lying Leopard TTouch						
Python TTouch						
Combined TTouch						
Abalone TTouch						
Llama TTouch						
Raccoon TTouch						
Bear TTouch						
Tiger TTouch						
Tarantula TTouch						
Hair Slides						
Lick of the Cow's Tongue						
Noah's March						
Zigzag TTouch						
Belly Lifts						
Mouth TTouch						
Ear TTouch						
Leg Circles: Front Legs						
Leg Circles: Back Legs						
TTouches on the Paws						
TTouches with the Paws						
Toenail Trimming						
Tail TTouch						

	DATE	DATE	DATE	DATE	DATE	DATE
LEADING EXERCISES						
With a flat collar						
Balance Leash						
Training with the Wand						
Introducing the Halti						
Wearing the Halti (without a leash)						
Leading with the Halti						
Half Body Wrap						
Body Wrap						
Double Diamond						
Dog Harness						
Homing Pigeon						

	DATE	DATE	DATE	DATE	DATE	DATE
THE CONFIDENCE COURSE						
The Labyrinth						
Boards and Platform						
Wire Mesh Surface						
Plastic Surface						
The Teeter-Totter (See-Saw)						
The A-Frame						
The Board Walk						
Poles						
The Star						
Cavaletti						
The Ladder						
The Tires						
Slalom Course						

Solving Behavior Problems

Leading Exercises over slippery surfaces increase a dog's self-confidence.

Your Dog is Fearful

Most dogs express fear with clear body language. They clamp their tails between their hind legs, and crouch in a submissive position. Other signs are nervous licking, urinating, rolling on to the back, a fixed stare, and a completely rigid body. Excessive fear can also lead to aggression; a dog may start to growl, snap, or even bite.

HOW TTOUCH WORK CAN HELP

Fearful dogs lack something very important: self-assurance and self-confidence. A dog with low self-esteem will often shun contact with other dogs and people. Life is not much fun for such a dog because he rarely relaxes. The TTouches can help overcome such problems. Through regular bodywork you can give your dog a better awareness of his body, thus increasing his self-esteem and self-confidence.

Start at your dog's head doing Ear TTouches, and connected Lying Leopard TTouches. If your dog tries to avoid your TTouch you can use the back of your hand, or switch to a different TTouch. Work your dog's whole body.

Lastly, work the hindquarters and tail. If he is nervous when you TTouch him on his hindquarters, we recommend using a Halti and the Wand. Stroke your dog with the Wand until he seems comfortable with it, showing no fear. After he is used to this, you should be able to change to doing Circular TTouches with your hand. Eating a treat can sometimes help a dog relax, which will reduce his fear. Speak to him in a soft tone of voice in order to calm him. I recommend five to ten minutes for a TTouch session. If you do this session regularly – once a day, for instance – you will find that you can considerably improve your dog's state of mind.

FOR MORE DETAILS

Ear TTouch p.58, Lying Leopard TTouch p.32, Llama TTouch p.37, Raccoon TTouch p.38, Body Wrap p.82, Halti p.76, Labyrinth p.94.

Your Dog is Aggressive

Dogs that tend to growl in inappropriate situations, bark aggressively, or even bite, can be helped with TTouches. An exception is aggressive behavior due to illness. In our view, aggression is usually triggered by insecurity, uncertainty about rank in the pack, pain, or fear. However, there are certain breeds of dogs that have been bred, or trained, to be aggressive.

Dogs learn to overcome their aggressiveness through training in the Labyrinth.

HOW TTOUCH TRAINING CAN HELP

Aggression is a complex problem that can have various causes and manifestations. Therefore, the dog that is aggressive needs to be approached in different ways. You must be sure to avoid threatening a dog that might become dangerous. Follow the basic rules of not looking a dog directly in the eye, unless he knows and trusts you. Approach a strange dog so he has to turn his head to look at you. Use the dog's name and talk to him in a friendly, soothing voice. Start the bodywork with the Wand if the dog seems to be uncertain about your hand. You can make Circular TTouches with the button end of the Wand on those areas of your dog's body that he feels comfortable having touched. Be content with a small amount of success, take your time, and do not demand too much of your dog.

If you notice that your dog is enjoying the TTouch with the Wand and you have gained his trust you can put a Body Wrap on him and start doing the usual TTouches with your hands. The Body Wrap and, in some cases, the Double Diamond, are very useful for aggressive dogs because they give them a secure experience of their own bodies. In addition, using the Double Diamond gives you more control of the dog.

Start the Leading Exercises and the groundwork with a Halti as soon as possible, because through this work your dog can learn to overcome his instinctive fearful reaction. He will learn to think by concentrating on specific tasks, and not be distracted as easily as before. The experience of success will make him happier and more confident. When you are working with a dog that is aggressive toward dogs, it is a good idea to lead him over the obstacles with other dogs (at a safe distance), or, with a dog that is hostile toward cats or other animals as well, do bodywork with these other animals nearby. This will help your dog overcome his impulse to attack them.

Trainers who are experienced in working with people-aggressive dogs report great success with Tellington TTouch work. However, please do not work with such animals unless you have a lot of experience. Note: a muzzle can be an extremely useful safety tool if you are uncertain about a dog's temperament.

FOR MORE DETAILS
Clouded Leopard TTouch p.28, Lying Leopard TTouch p.32, Mouth TTouch p.54, Body Wrap p.82, Halti p.76, Labyrinth p.94.

Your Dog is Nervous

Belly Lifts with a towel enhance a dog's breathing and relax his abdominal and his back muscles.

A nervous dog is restless, breathes fast and irregularly, pants, and is sometimes hard to control. Some dogs are nervous by nature, but often nervousness is the result of stress (just as it is in humans).

HOW TTOUCH WORK CAN HELP
TTouches are great for a nervous dog because he learns to relax by releasing tension from his body. This newfound ability to relax will later occur even in stressful situations. Start by doing Circular TTouches on his whole body and concentrate on those areas that the dog enjoys having touched. In order to help a dog regulate his breathing you can try Ear TTouches and Belly Lifts. The Body Wrap and the Mouth TTouch are also appropriate for nervous dogs – the Mouth TTouch being especially helpful because this TTouch affects the limbic system in the brain that controls emotion. A seldom-recognized sign of nervousness is extremely fast, nonstop tail wagging. Before the dog will be able to relax you need to hold the tail absolutely still with a gentle, firm pressure of your hand on the top of the root of the tail.

FOR MORE DETAILS
Clouded Leopard TTouch p.28, Lying Leopard TTouch p.32, Mouth TTouch p.54, Belly Lift p.52, Body Wrap p.82, Halti p.76, The Labyrinth p.94.

Your Dog Barks Uncontrollably

A constantly barking dog is exhausting, not only for the people around him, but also for the dog because he puts himself under permanent stress. As long as his behavior is controlled by emotion rather than reason, this sort of dog is not responsive, and, therefore, incapable of learning. The Tellington TTouch Method can help you resolve such a no-win situation.

HOW TTOUCH WORK CAN HELP

One of the basic rules of TTouch training is to have a clear mental image of the behavior you want. Therefore, I suggest that you walk up to your barking dog and imagine, or visualize, him being quiet. Ask him to sit, and start with the Ear TTouch. As you sense him getting calmer, slow down your Ear Slides accordingly. Do Lying Leopard TTouches on his whole body to further quiet him.

The Mouth TTouch is also very helpful for constant, chronic barking cases, because TTouches on the mouth affect the limbic system in the brain that controls emotion. Do not wait until your dog barks before starting the Mouth TTouch, but work with him at any time. You can achieve a major change in behavior without any direct association with the barking.

Doing Raccoon TTouch circles on the stub of a tail that has been docked can alleviate tension caused by resulting "phantom limb" pain.

FOR MORE DETAILS

Ear TTouch p.58, Lying Leopard TTouch p.32, Mouth TTouch p.54, Tail TTouch p.70, Halti p.76.

Your Dog Suffers Separation Anxiety

By nature, your dog is a member of a pack, so it is not unreasonable for him to get restless and become anxious whenever you, or your family, leave him alone. Nevertheless, dogs can learn to be by themselves for certain periods of time, or to accept other people as temporary caretakers.

HOW TTOUCH WORK CAN HELP

Most dogs that suffer from separation anxiety are young, fearful, or insecure. Therefore it is important to boost your dog's self-confidence through bodywork. It is also useful to get him used to other people and learn to trust them. Gentle Lying Leopard TTouches on his entire body are helpful by developing self-confidence and self-control. The Body Wrap is another useful tool because it gives your dog a feeling of security and protection.

The warmth of the hand doing the Lying Leopard TTouch relaxes body and soul.

FOR MORE DETAILS

Lying Leopard TTouch p.32, Tail TTouch p.70, Body Wrap p.82.

Your Dog is Difficult to Walk on the Leash

You should do specific Leading Exercises if your dog pulls on the leash, runs in all directions, or lags behind.

HOW TTOUCH WORK CAN HELP

The Tellington TTouch Method offers several solutions. Leading Exercises with a Halti is the treatment of choice if your dog pulls on the leash. The Halti allows you to lead your dog with clear signals. The Balance Leash and the Double Diamond are also helpful because they assist in controlling the dog's front legs and hindquarters. When leading a rambunctious dog use the Wand to calm him by stroking him.

FOR MORE DETAILS

Halti p.76, Balance Leash p.74, Double Diamond p.86, Body Wrap p.82, Wand p.75.

Your Dog Chews Everything

The Mouth TTouch also helps a dog overcome boredom.

Though common in a puppy, chewing shoes, furniture, or other objects not specifically given to him, can become a very bad habit if it continues. In most cases, excessive chewing is either a sign of teething, or is caused by a lack of exercise, stimulation, or as a result of being left alone.

HOW TTOUCH WORK CAN HELP

Try the Mouth TTouch since I have found it solves the teething problem. Do tiny, firm Raccoon TTouches on the gums above the teeth to relieve discomfort. Two or three five-minute sessions will alleviate inappropriate chewing. (In addition, you can offer safe toys to chew on.) With the Mouth TTouch, a dog will be able to pass the teething stage more quickly and easily. Sometimes it helps to perform the Mouth TTouch with an ice-cold washcloth or flannel. A few five-minute treatments are often sufficient to stop a dog from chewing.

FOR MORE DETAILS

Mouth TTouch p.54.

Your Dog is Anxious About Riding in the Car

Most dogs love riding in the car. However, if your dog has had a bad experience in the car – becoming sick, or being scared, for example – traveling in the car can become a problem.

HOW TTOUCH WORK CAN HELP

If your dog tends to get carsick do the Ear TTouches. Ear Slides will prevent vomiting, or drooling, and will calm him. If your dog barks in the car or runs around nervously, ask a friend to drive while you put a Halti on him to keep him under control. However, be sure to practice putting on the Halti and leading your dog with it, before you use it in the car. Do a few minutes of bodywork in the car before starting the engine. As a next step, continue the bodywork while the car is driven slowly with frequent stops. In the next session, increase the length of the drive gradually and ask the driver to speed up as long as the dog remains calm. Normally, it will only take a few exercises for your dog to become comfortable. A Body Wrap can also be helpful. Overall, for safety, it is better to keep dogs confined in a car – for travel I recommend a seat belt, or the use of a crate.

Circular TTouches on the ears can reduce carsickness and nervousness.

FOR MORE DETAILS

Ear TTouch p.58, Halti p.76, Body Wrap p.82.

Your Dog is Hyperactive

Some dogs are hyperactive from birth, while some breeds of animal are especially active. In our modern world it is often impossible to give every dog an appropriate amount of exercise. The TTouch can help reduce pent up energy so that the dog is better able to adjust to city life. However, you should always choose a breed that fits your lifestyle and needs. Of course, one way to make sure that your dog gets enough exercise is to hire a dog walker to do it for you, or take your dog to a park where dogs are allowed to gather and play together.

There are hyperactive dogs that, even after a long walk, extensive play, or all-out roughhousing, rest for only a short period of time. These dogs are usually nervous, not concentrating on one thing for any length of time. Sometimes an illness is the cause of such behavior (for example, allergies or a hyperthyroid condition) and

Groundwork in the Confidence Course, can help the hyperactive dog.

must be diagnosed and treated. Even in these cases however, the TTouches, Leading Exercises, and Confidence Course can be helpful.

HOW TTOUCH WORK CAN HELP

Any type of bodywork with the TTouches changes your dog's behavior. Sometimes, just a few sessions lead to amazing results.

The Ear TTouch and the Combined TTouch applied to the whole body have proven especially effective for hyperactivity. You can use the Clouded Leopard TTouch to create new body awareness, and a relaxed state. Stroking the body with the Zigzag TTouch can help relax your dog. Also, try the Body Wrap, Leading Exercises, and groundwork with the Confidence Course.

FOR MORE DETAILS

Combined TTouch p.35, Clouded Leopard TTouch p.28, Zigzag TTouch p.51, Body Wrap p.82, Halti p.76, Confidence Course p.92.

TTouch Resources

USEFUL ADDRESSES

For further information about TTouch Training, TTEAM, Animal
Ambassadors, Tellington TTouch Practitioners near you, Tellington
TTouch Training Tools, or other publications by Linda Tellington-
Jones, contact one of the following Tellington TTouch offices:

United States
TTEAM & TTouch Training
  Headquarters
Linda Tellington-Jones
PO Box 3793
Santa Fe, NM 87501
Tel: 1-800-854-TEAM (8326)
      1-505-455-2945
Fax: 1-505-455-7233
e-mail: info@tteam-ttouch.com
web: www.tellingtonttouch.com

United Kingdom
Sarah Fisher
South Hill House
Radford, Bath
Somerset BA3 1QQ
Tel: 01761 471 182
Fax: 01761 472 982
e-mail: sarahfisher@msn.com

Canada
Robyn Hood
5435 Rochdell Rd.
Vernon, BC
V1B 3E8
Tel: 1-800-255-2336
      1-250-545-2336
Fax: 1-250-545-9116
e-mail: ttouch@home.com

Australia
Andy Robertson
28 Calderwood Rd.
Gaiston NSW 02159
Tel: 0404 255496
e-mail: ttouch@cia.com.au

South Africa
Eugenie Chopin
PO Box 729
Strathaven 2031
Tel: 27-11-8843156
Fax: 27-11-7831515
e-mail: echopin@icon.co.za

Germany
Bibi Degn
Hassel 4
D-57589 Pracht
Tel: 02682-8886
Fax: 02682-6683
e-mail: bibi@tteam.de
web: www.tteam.de

Austria
Martin Lasser
Anningerstr. 18
A-2353 Guntramsdorf
Tel: 02236 47040
e-mail: TTeam.office@aon.at
web: www.tteamaustria.at

The Netherlands
Nelleke Deen
Staverenstraat 10 B
NL-3043 RS Rotterdam
Tel & Fax: 01041 52594
e-mail: nelleke@dest.demon.nl

Sweden
Christina Drangel
Svavelsovagen 11
184 92 Rydbo
Saltsjobad
Tel & Fax: 08-540-27488
e-mail: jmpette@ibm.net

Switzerland
Doris Süess-Schröttle
Mascot
Ausbildungszentrum AG
CH-8566 Neuwilen
Tel: 071 6991825
Fax: 071 6991827
e-mail: mascot@swissonlone.ch

TELLINGTON TTOUCH TRAINING TOOLS

These dog training tools can be ordered from TTouch Training offices and on-line at www.tellingtonttouch.com:

- TTouch Wand
- Nylon and leather leashes
- Jelly scrubbers
- Snoot Loop™ halters
- Haltis™

NEWSLETTER

Keep up-to-date with all the news about TTEAM and the Tellington TTouch by subscribing to *TTEAM Connections*, a bimonthly, 24-page newsletter. It's dedicated to educating people about the TTEAM and TTouch methods along with other complementary ideas to help increase your understanding of animals and improve behavior, well-being, and performance. The newsletter includes: articles by Linda Tellington-Jones and Robyn Hood; case histories and letters from readers; and questions with answers from Linda and Robyn. Contributing writers include TTEAM and TTouch Practitioners and Instructors, as well as people from complementary fields.

TTOUCH TRAINING

Workshops

There are TTouch Training Practitioners through the world with over 150 in the United States and Canada, and 20 in England. If you would like to bring the magic of TTouch to your club or local dog group, you can host a two-day TTouch Workshop for companion animals in your area. All you need is a group of enthusiastic people and TTouch Training will send one of its highly qualified trainers to teach you and your group the proven benefits of using TTouch on dogs. The workshop will cover the basic principles and techniques used in TTouch. Typically, you will learn how to:

- Learn the primary TTouches and when to apply them
- Deepen your relationship with your dog or cat
- Enhance the willingness and ability of your animal to learn
- Relieve symptoms of stress, such as excessive licking and chewing
- Help alleviate aggression and timidity in your dog
- Stop your dog from pulling on the leash
- Slow the effects of arthritis and aging
- Accelerate recovery from surgery or injury in conjunction with veterinary care
- Help your animals with common problems like jumping up, barking, scratching, timidity, separation anxiety, and many more

How to Become a Tellington TTouch Practitioner for Dogs, Cats, and Other Animal Companions

The certification program for TTouch Practitioner for dogs, cats, and other animal companions is designed for people who want to work with animals on a full or part-time basis and for people who just want to share the benefits of TTouch with their own animals. There are hundreds of professional TTouch Practitioners all over the world. Some work full-time with private clients, many do TTouch part-time in addition to their other jobs, and some incorporate what they have learned into their work with animals in shelters, obedience schools, veterinary clinics, and zoos. The rewards of this training program include an inspiring way to relate to animals, and for many, a new appreciation and understanding of ourselves and our own species.

The certification program to become a TTouch Practitioner takes approximately two years and requires a considerable investment of time and effort. The program is part-time and consists of six sessions (three per year) each lasting between five and seven days.

During the two-year professional training and certification program, you will:

- Experience ways of working with dogs, cats, birds, and other pets that are unique and rewarding, and can change your life
- Acquire easy-to-use skills to deal with common behavior and health-related problems
- Use techniques to increase performance and reduce stress in show, obedience, agility, *schutzhund*, and trial dogs
- Work with shelter animals to help them adapt more easily to new environments
- Learn how to help animals recover more quickly from surgery and injury
- Understand how TTouch inspires understanding and compassion for all life

For more information or to enroll in the TTouch Practitioner program, contact:

TTEAM and TTouch Training Headquarters
P.O. Box 3793
Santa Fe, NM 87501-0793
Tel: 1-800-854-8326
Fax: 1-505-455-7233
e-mail: info@tteam-ttouch.com
web: www.tellingtonttouch.com

ALSO BY LINDA TELLINGTON-JONES

Books

Getting in TTouch: Understand and Influence Your Horse's Personality (published in the UK as *Getting in Touch with Horses*)

Improve Your Horse's Well-Being: A Step-by-Step Guide to TTouch and TTEAM Training

Let's Ride with Linda Tellington-Jones: Fun and TTeamwork with Your Horse or Pony

The Tellington-TTouch: A Breakthrough Technique to Train and Care for Your Favorite Animal

The Tellington-Jones Equine Awareness Method

Videos

Unleash Your Dog's Potential: Getting in TTouch with Your Canine Friend (US version); available in PAL format as *Getting in Touch with Your Dog: Unleash Your Dog's Potential* from Kenilworth Press

The TTouch of Magic for Horses

The TTouch of Magic for Dogs

The TTouch of Magic for Cats

Haltering Your Foal
Handling Mares and Stallions
Learning Exercises Part 1
Learning Exercises Part 2
Riding with Awareness
Solving Riding Problems with TTEAM: From the Ground
Solving Riding Problems with TTEAM: In the Saddle
Starting a Young Horse
TTouch for Dressage
Tellington-Touch for Happier, Healthier Dogs
Tellington-Touch for Happier, Healthier Cats

TTouch Glossary

ABALONE TTOUCH The TTouch done with a completely flat hand, which moves the skin in a circle.

A-FRAME Two climbing walls, which are joined together to form a roof-like obstacle.

BALANCE LEASH A leading leash that is placed across the dog's chest and enhances balance.

BEAR TTOUCH A circular TTouch that is performed with the nails of curved fingers.

BELLY LIFT For relaxation, the dog's belly is lifted gently with a towel or with the hand.

BOARDS A board, or boards, placed on the ground, which act as obstacles to prepare a dog for the Board Walk. It improves a dog's self-confidence and balance.

BODY WRAP The Body Wrap can be wrapped in many different ways. It enhances a dog's awareness of his own body, thus giving him confidence in himself.

CAVALETTI Usually a sequence of raised poles over which a dog can run, and jump.

CLOUDED LEOPARD TTOUCH This basic form of the TTouch is a circular movement with the slightly curved hand that moves the skin in a circle one-and-a-quarter times around.

COMBINED TTOUCH A combination of either the Lying Leopard TTouch or Abalone TTouch together with the Python TTouch.

BOARD WALK A raised narrow board that trains attentiveness and balance.

DOUBLE DIAMOND A special "body rope" for dogs that gives the handler control over aggressive and hyperactive dogs.

EAR TTOUCH A stroking, or circular, TTouch on the ear. Stimulating the acupressure points on the ear has a positive effect on the whole body, and can prevent shock after an accident.

HAIR SLIDES Even slides along the dog's fur, which relax and improve circulation.

HALTI A special head collar for dogs that allows the handler to control the dog's head more easily than a leash.

HARNESS A dog-friendly harness that does not put any pressure on the neck.

JOURNEY OF THE HOMING PIGEON A leading position in which the dog is led from both sides.

LABYRINTH A ground obstacle made from 6 long poles. It increases a dog's concentration, and consequently, his ability to learn.

LADDER Used as a ground obstacle to teach coordination.

LEG CIRCLES Even, alternating circles with the front and back legs, relax tension and improve balance and coordination.

LICK OF THE COW'S TONGUE A stimulating TTouch consisting of long, diagonal strokes.

LLAMA TTOUCH A TTouch done with the back of the hand, which is less threatening than an open hand to a sensitive and/or fearful dog.

LYING LEOPARD TTOUCH A variation on the Clouded Leopard TTouch. Your hand is flattened somewhat, the fingers perform the circle, and the palm produces relaxing warmth.

MOUTH TTOUCH TTouches on and around the muzzle, and on the lips and gums. The Mouth TTouch stimulates the limbic system in the brain, which controls the emotions.

NOAH'S MARCH A long, stroking TTouch over the entire body that introduces or concludes a treatment session.

OBSTACLES Work with obstacles (the Confidence Course) improves a dog's trust, obedience, and balance.

PAW TTOUCH Small, Circular TTouches on the paws, "ground" a dog and helps him overcome fear.

PLASTIC SURFACE An obstacle that simulates any slippery surface, and teaches balance and sure-footedness.

POLES Name of an obstacle, and versatile equipment used to make the Star and the Labyrinth.

PYTHON TTOUCH The TTouch performed with both hands to move the skin. It has a relaxing effect, especially on the legs.

RACCOON TTOUCH A very light TTouch for sensitive areas. The tips of the fingers perform circular movements with the lightest pressure.

SLALOM Running around poles or cones, enhances a dog's agility.

SNOOT LOOP Is similar to the Halti, but more adjustable.

STAR Consists of poles that are placed in a semi-circle and raised on one end.

TAIL TTOUCH TTouches that are performed on the tail&circles, bending, pulling. This TTouch relaxes a dog's body posture.

TARANTULAS PULLING THE PLOW For this gentle version of the skin roll, both hands "walk" over the body like a spider.

TEETER-TOTTER (SEE-SAW) A ground obstacle that improves a dog's balance.

TELLINGTON-TTOUCH METHOD. The complete system consists of the TTouches, Leading Exercises, and the Confidence Course.

TIGER TTOUCH A TTouch that is performed with the nails of the fingers, which are curved and spread apart so that the hand looks like a paw.

TIRES/TYRES Car tires are very versatile tools to use as, or with, obstacles.

TTEAM Acronym for the Tellington-Jones Equine Awareness Method. In the beginning, Linda Tellington-Jones developed her method for horses; now it is used on many other animals. Now, TTEAM can also stand for the Tellington-Jones Every Animal Method.

TTOUCH Acronym for the Tellington TTouch Method. It also refers to an individual TTouch (The Clouded Leopard TTouch, for example). TTouches make up the bodywork section of the Tellington TTouch Method.

TTOUCHES WITH THE PAW Circular movements done with the dog's paw.

WAND This is used to stroke the body of a nervous, or aggressive, dog from a safe distance, and show direction.

WIRE MESH SURFACE A ground obstacle that improves a dog's sure-footedness.

ZIGZAG TTOUCH A long, stroking TTouch performed in a zigzag motion across the body.

Index

Page numbers in **bold** indicate main discussions; those in *italics* indicate photographs